Low-Intensity Cognitive Bel Therapy; A Psychological Wellbeing Practitioner (PWP) Handbook.

David Kaneria

APA Reference:
Kaneria, D. (2022). *Low-Intensity Cognitive Behaviour Therapy; A Psychological Wellbeing Practitioner (PWP) Handbook*. Kindle Direct Publishing.

Harvard Reference:
Kaneria, D. (2022). *Low-Intensity Cognitive Behaviour Therapy; A Psychological Wellbeing Practitioner (PWP) Handbook*. Kindle Direct Publishing, UK.

About The Author:

David Kaneria is a Senior Psychological Wellbeing Practitioner (sPWP) currently working within IAPT in Hertfordshire. I qualified from Essex university as a Psychological Wellbeing Practitioner in 2020.
Prior to this I qualified from my bachelors degree studying Abnormal and Clinical Psychology at Anglia Ruskin in 2013 and my Masters in Cognitive and Clinical Neuroscience also at Anglia Ruskin in 2015.

Why I Wrote This Book:

The road to becoming a PWP is difficult. Ask any trainee PWP this and they will most likely all agree. Between working, studying and the multiple assessments, you are expected to become highly proficient in delivering low-intensity CBT in a very short space of time. You will be expected to go from a lecture on a treatment, to the next day or week using this protocol with a real life patient. The pressure and demand of this can be scary, stressful but the effort leads to a highly rewarding job.

I was highly fortunate in my journey to becoming a PWP. My partner was already a qualified PWP and had taught me all the basics of the job before I even had my first interview. This gave me a huge advantage during the interview, lectures and on the job. I felt more confident, it reduced the demands of the job and made the training much less stressful compared to my peers; who often reflected on my perceived competence compared to them. And that is why I wanted to write this guide. I wanted to pass on this advantage to as many aspiring therapists as possible. The more prepared you are before you start, the less stressful you will find the job, and in my opinion the better clinical outcomes for patients.

Contents:

Purpose Of The Book:

The purpose of this book is not to replace the PWP training in any way.

This book is designed to guide those who wish to become a PWP to have more insight into what the job entails, and provide you with knowledge that can help you stand out in the interview process. It is also designed to help those who have been accepted onto the course and prepare you for the university course required to become a qualified PWP.

With this in mind, the book will not be an exhaustive step by step guide to all the job entails, with full citations or critique. But will give a good outline of the job, assessments, diagnosis and treatments you will be required to undertake during the job.

How To Use This Book:
It is recommended that you read through the book in order to give you a complete understanding. However some sections will be more or less relevant depending on the stage you are in (interview or training). During each section we will put a seed icon near important points for those who are prior to the interview stage for important points to know for the interviews. For PWP trainees beginning or during the course we will use an apple icon .

The PWP role and the university course is continually evolving and there can be discrepancies based on which university you go to. This book will provide the basic outline. It is important to always follow the current guidelines from both your university and your service as they will always override what might be stated in this guide.

The contents of this book relate to the UK IAPT training. Therefore most of this book will not be as relevant to outside of the UK.

All models and diagrams can freely be used assuming reference to this guide is made.

What Is A Psychological Wellbeing Practitioner (PWP):

A PWP is a type of therapist who has received specific training to work with those who are experiencing common mental health problems such as anxiety and depression. They work and are employed as a part of the NHS's Improving Access to Psychological Therapies (IAPT) services; which as the name suggests aims to improve access to therapy on the NHS. PWP's also work as a part of a wider team of healthcare professionals including high-intensity CBT Therapists, Senior Clinicians and supervisors. And depending on the service in question, this can include counsellors, employment support services and other specialist NHS services, or external organisations such as charities (ie MIND).

PWP Job Role:
The role of a PWP is varied but compasses three main areas: clinical, administrative and continued professional development/training.

Clinical:
The average PWP will conduct initial assessments on referrals to discover a patient's main problem and to screen for suitability within the service. Often a PWP does at least nine of these types of assessments a week with the average assessment lasting 45 minutes.

PWP's also offer treatment sessions using low intensity CBT techniques. These sessions often last 30 minutes. Most services typically offer these sessions over the telephone, as compared to face to face. Since the Covid pandemic, virtual online sessions are increasingly becoming a popular alternative. Typically, a PWP will offer approximately twenty of these sessions a week depending on the service requirements.

Administrative:
PWP are tasked with many administrative duties. First being effective management of their own caseloads. A skill which can take much time to master but very important due to the high caseloads and volume of the role. Caseloads range based on your service but often can exceed 60-100 patients.

Other duties include
- Clear and accurate notetaking of every session or interaction with patients.
- Creating and sending letters to patients.
- Discharging patients.
- Bring cases to discuss with their supervisor during weekly case-management supervision.
- Working with other members of the team to ensure appropriate step-ups and step-down procedures based on a stepped care approach. More on this later in this chapter.

Continued Professional Development/Training:
As a trainee PWP, you are required to fulfil the academic requirements of the role. Failing this requirement can result in termination of your employment contract. After qualification, you are expected to engage in continued personal and professional development in your clinical practice.

During the first year training to become a PWP you are required to undergo a training course at the university alongside working.
Typically one day a week at university. One day a week home studying. And three days a week working within an IAPT service.

The university training will involve lectures, a lot of role plays (and I really mean a lot), writing reflective outcomes, multiple essays and recorded (and often dreaded by trainee's) Objective Clinical Structured Examinations (OCSE's).

The university course consists of three modules:
Module 1: Engagement And Assessment (Of Patients With Common Mental Health Problems).
Module 2: Evidence-Based Low-Intensity Treatment (For Common Mental Health Disorders).
Module 3: Values, Employment And Context.

At the start of the course you will have a highly reduced caseload compared to a qualified PWP. This will slowly increase as the year progresses. By the third module this will increase to 60-80% of a qualified PWP.

Outcomes: For each module you typically have three outcome essays to write. These relate to what you have learnt. *And most importantly, how you personally apply this to your work. This is designed to be a reflective essay so ensure you don't be descriptive and write about the theory only. They are designed to ensure you practice this in reality and are looking for you to demonstrate this with examples and personal reflection.*

Exams: Each university has the discretion to change the assessment types but they do require a mixture of OSCE's, recordings and Essays. So one cohort may have an OSCE for an initial assessment (IA), while the next cohort's OSCE is on a treatment session. Regardless of if it is an OCSE or a recording you will write a reflective essay on your performance.
Roleplays: During the university course you will engage in a lot of roleplays to improve your skills. This can often be a source of stress when the course begins, but by the end of it you will be very proficient in them.

Portfolio: Throughout each module you will be expected to keep a portfolio to record your clinical work in service. This includes reflective outcomes on your performance. This will be marked by the university who will also liaise with your service to ensure you are working competently with patients.

Interview Tip: Know what the job role is before your interview.
Key points:
- *PWP's assess patients. Read our chapter on initial assessments for more information.*
- *PWP's offer guided self help as treatment. Read our chapter on treatments for more information.*
- *You will work while going to university and be expected to keep a portfolio.*

What Is CBT:

PWP are also known as low intensity CBT practitioners. CBT is a melding of two main schools of psychology; Behaviourism and Cognitive therapy.

This book will not go into any detail about the history of CBT. There are many great books which could do this better justice than I; and the topic could be a whole book in itself. But we will focus on the aspects needed for working within IAPT.

Behavioural: Behaviourism is the idea that all behaviours are acquired through conditioning which occurs when individuals interact with their environment. Certain cues or signals start to shape action. For example, if every time a child tried to speak it was shouted at, the child may learn to not speak as often for fear of being reprimanded.

Cognitive therapy: The Cognitive approach believes that it is what we think about our environment, situation or the self, that causes dysfunction. Going back to the child who was shouted at for talking. A Cognitive approach might state that the child has learnt something about **why** they were being told off. And stops talking due to these thoughts.

For example "I never have anything interesting to say", "I am stupid", "I must be bad for being told off" or "Only bad children get shouted at, so I must be a bad child".

Key Principles of CBT:

- CBT states that three areas underlie mental health:
1) Cognitions: CBT states that situations, and events are interpreted incorrectly which often cause impaired functioning and affect mood.
2) Behaviours: The way we act can influence our mood. Therefore, if we change how to act, we will change how we feel.
3) Autonomic (Physical feelings): The way we feel physically can influence both our cognitions and behaviours.

- These three areas are all interlinked and dysfunction in one area can affect the other areas. This often can cause a vicious cycle that causes the dysfunction to maintain itself.

- CBT focuses on "*maintenance cycles*": Understanding what is maintaining mental disorders is key in improving mental health.

Interview Tip: You don't have to be an expert in CBT before you apply for the job. But knowing the three areas above will be a great help. Use these three areas to show your understanding of CBT if a question was to come up.

Other principles of CBT:

- Semi structured: CBT is often a semi structured therapy. An agenda is set for each session in a collaborative way with the patient.

- Collaborative: CBT is highly collaborative and places a large importance on working with the patient with the aims of guided self discovery. It is said that CBT can not be "done to a patient, only **with** a patient".

- Personalised: CBT uses formulations and models of various mental disorders but always remembers patients are unique and aims to see how these models fit the patient as an individual.

- Time limited: CBT is designed to be time limited. On the NHS, CBT is a short term therapy. A set number of sessions is often given. With the aim being to give the patient the skills and self reliance to make changes in their life which extend beyond the therapy.

- Scientific: CBT is scientific. It relies on research, clinical trials and established treatment protocols. It aims to only use evidenced based treatments.

What Is IAPT:

The "Improving Access to Psychological Therapies" (IAPT) programme began in 2008 and aimed to transform and improve accessibility to psychological treatment of anxiety disorders and depression in England.

Currently the NHS *"Five Year Forward View Of Mental Health"* plan aims to increase the number of patients seen by 380,000 per year to reach 1.9 million a year by 2023/24.

IAPT services aim to:
1) Provide evidence-based psychology therapies via the use of fully trained and accredited practitioners.

2) Conduct "Routine Outcome Monitoring" so that patients progress can be monitored. This also allows for anonymised and published performance statistics.

3) Regular and outcome focused supervisions so that practitioners are continually improving and delivering high quality care.

Priorities for services also include:
1) To expand services to increase access.
2) Focus on patients with long term health conditions (LTCs) to improve mental wellbeing.
3) Support people to find or stay in work.
4) Improve quality of life for patients.

To achieve this ambitious goal of improving access IAPT is continually hiring new PWP's. The demand for PWP's has never been higher. However, the competition is tough for training places and the course can be challenging.

Interview Tip: Knowing one or two statistics about IAPT will put you above most candidates. Remembering either recovery rates or the amount of patients seen a year is advised.

Stepped Care Model:

Mental Health in England is based on the *"Stepped Care Model"*. This model is built on the principle that patients should be offered the **least intrusive intervention for their needs**. When treatment is not effective or appropriate then the patient will be moved on to the **next step to receive further support**. Patient's can also be moved down a step where appropriate. Often called "A step up/stepping up" or "A step down/stepping down".
This is to ensure that the NHS's limited resources are allocated where they are needed.

For IAPT purposes only four steps are relevant.
- Step 1: is primary care services such as GP's. This step is designed to detect the possibility for psychological support. GP's will refer patients to IAPT and/or try pharmacological interventions.
- Step 2: refers to the use of guided self help within IAPT. This will be delivered by a PWP or in some cases an Assistant Psychologist or other qualified therapists.
- Step 3: refers to formal CBT within IAPT. This will be delivered by a High Intensity CBT therapist who are accredited by the BABCP (The British Association for Behavioural and Cognitive Psychotherapies).
- Step 4: Refers to NHS secondary care services. This will be when the patient is too high risk for IAPT in terms of sucide. Or for when the patient has very severe symptoms or difficulties IAPT is not commissioned for (such as complex trauma, personality disorders), or for when repeated treatment has not been successful at step 3.

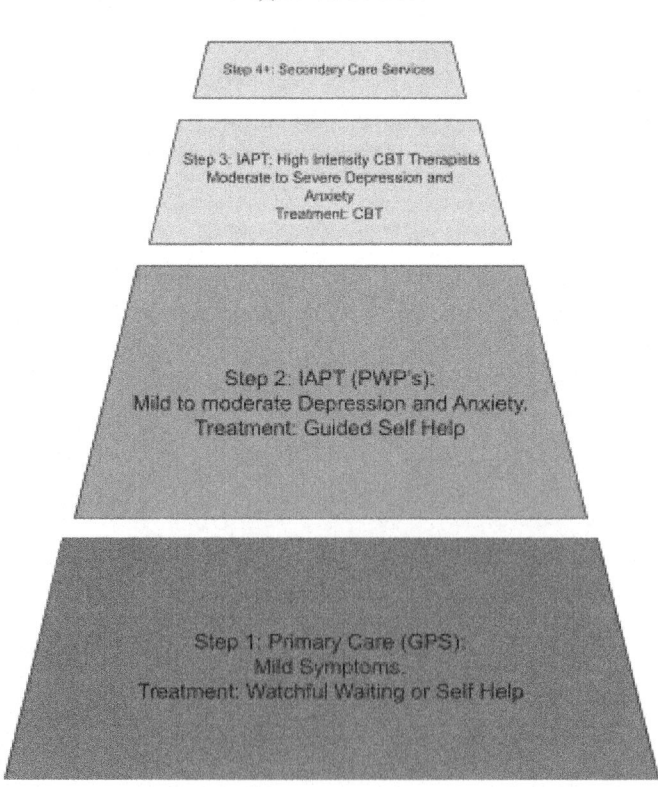

Figure 1: Stepped Care model

Due to the stepped care model there are two types of CBT used within IAPT:

The first being Low intensity CBT (also known as Guided Self Help) and the other being Brief High Intensity CBT.

Low Intensity CBT (Step 2):
- Is typically delivered by a PWP.
- Utilises self-help materials.
- Averages at six hours or less of contact time.
- Each contact is typically 30 minutes or less.
- Typically has a lower evidence base due to its recent creation for IAPT.

Brief High Intensity CBT (Step 3):
- This will be delivered by a CBT therapist who is accredited by the BABCP (The British Association for Behavioural and Cognitive Psychotherapies).
- Does not rely on self-help materials, instead focusing on worksheets selected for the individual patient.
- Approximately 12-14 hours of contact time.
- Each contact typically lasts 60 minutes or less.
- Uses the traditional rich CBT evidence base.
- Has 50% or less of the traditional contact time of traditional CBT.

Interview Tip:
Demonstrating an awareness of stepped care in an interview will show you have a good knowledge of how IAPT works. You don't need to know in detail how it works.
The basics:
The patient will have an assessment when referred to an IAPT service with a PWP. Based on this assessment the patient will either be:
1. *"Stepped down" and sent back to the referer if not suitable.*
2. *"Taken into step 2" and offered guided self help.*
3. *"Stepped up to step 3" for CBT.*
4. *"Stepped out of service" to step 4 or elsewhere.*

Trainee Tip:
Attempt to get a good understanding of this process. It will be the backbone of your job.

Interview Process And Tips:

If you have already secured a job then skip to the end chapter.

This guide will not go into detail about interviews in particular. Providing example questions would give an unfair advantage and largely be unhelpful since every service across the UK will be looking for slightly different things.

Throughout the guide in each section I will provide the knowledge you need to make you stand out in the interview. Even showing an awareness of the job will place you in a much better position to get the job.

Interviews often have two distinctive parts: a roleplay and standard interview questions.

First you will often be required to perform a 10 minute roleplay. Just hearing this often fills an applicant with terror and will put off many applicants from applying. However, the role play is often very easy and less stressful once you have practised a few. This role play will be about assessing a patient. The interviewers do not expect you to do a flawless assessment or even be aware of how. But they will be looking at your common factor skills. Read our chapter on this under core competences for detailed information.

A good roleplay should include:
- Gathering information on the patient's main problem. If you use the funnelling method used in the core competences you will appear very proficient.
- Empathy towards the patient. Use empathy statements from the core competences.
- An awareness of risk. See the book section on this. You don't need to be an expert. Just show an awareness.

After the role play you may be asked to **critically reflect** on your performance. This is a perfect opportunity to shine. You do not yet have the skills needed to do an assessment. Name the skills from the core competences or IA chapters and show that you are aware of them even if you didn't manage to do them. Critically reflecting isn't about saying you did everything perfectly. Acknowledge what went wrong in your roleplay as well as what you did well. **Don't just say you are nervous** so your role play didn't go to plan (every interviewee is equally as nervous).

The interview questions will vary, but knowing the things below will help you answer any question

- Values: Knowing the NHS values or the values of the trust you are applying for is a must. They often match you against this. A question can directly ask about this.
- What the job is: You may be asked to demonstrate you know what you are applying for. Reading this guide will help answer any of these questions. Knowing a bit about assessments and name dropping the treatments will put you way ahead of the pack.
- Knowledge of IAPT: Know a bit about IAPT. Read our section on this and know a few figures. Ie. How many patients does IAPT see a year? Know what the 5-year plan is.
- What are your future plans: Many people use the PWP job as a gateway to getting onto the psychology doctorate or becoming a High Intensity Therapist. Great, nothing wrong with that. But the service may be looking and hoping for a PWP who will stay in the job for longer. Maybe also consider a supervisor or a senior PWP job when answering this question.
- A knowledge and respect for diversity.

- Awareness of assessing and managing risk can also be in interview questions as well as the roleplay. See the section under module one for this.
- Flexibility and ability to think of your feet: You may be asked a question to see how you solve a simple problem.
- Personal skills: This is the same for any interview. What are you good at? What are you bad at? Look up typical interview skills and questions. Below are some key skills you will need for IAPT.
  1. Time management: PWPs manage their own caseloads so this is a must
  2. IT skills: you will be required to use patient databases to write digital notes, organise your cases and book in patients.
  3. Professionalism: You will be working for the NHS in a patient facing role. This is important.
  4. Academic skills: You will be at university, meeting deadlines and writing essays.
  5. Stress management: This will be a high pressure job. The panel needs to know how you relax and will handle this.

You may also get an example situation and be asked questions based on it. This can be to assess your knowledge of disorders and diagnosis, awareness of risk, ability to be flexible and think quickly. The only way to prepare for this would be to read this guide and remember the key points. No panel will expect an applicant to know everything. So no need to memorise the whole book.

Module One: Engagement and Assessment of Patients with Common Mental Health Problems:

Module one aims to teach PWP how to undertake screening assessments in the form of patient-centred interviews (often called the Initial Assessment/Appointment or simply shortened to the letters "IA"). This assessment is designed to identify the patients main difficulties, symptoms, goals and suitability for treatment. This interview will also include the assessment of the risk the person poses to themselves or others.

This module will teach you how to engage with patients and establish a therapeutic rapport to effectively gather information and aid the patient in collaboratively choosing a treatment programme. This will develop a set of "common factor" skills and competences to aid with this.

On this module you will gain knowledge of mental health disorders and a brief understanding of the evidence-based therapeutic options available. You will be taught to communicate this knowledge in a clear way so that patients can make informed treatment choices.

Knowledge will be learnt through a combination of lectures, seminars, reading and independent study. These skills will be put into practice almost immediately in service and therefore have a high focus on practical skills development.

This module will be assessed with a mixture of OSCEs, essays and recordings. You will also be asked to complete a portfolio demonstrating hours worked, three written outcomes regarding your practice. This will be supervised by your service supervisor and marked by the university.

Initial Assessments (IA):

This chapter is dedicated to outlining what an initial assessment (IA) looks like. As mentioned in our previous chapters, most qualified PWP will do approximately 9 of these appointments a week. Initial assessments are often the first thing you will learn on the course and you will be expected to start doing them within a few weeks of starting the course.

Interview stage:
During the interview for a PWP job you may be asked to roleplay an assessment. You will not be expected to know how to complete a full assessment at this stage. They will be looking at your ability to gather information and awareness of the process. Your common factor skills outlined in our chapter on Core Competences will be important at this stage. Use the funnelling method outlined in this chapter for extra marks. Although no interviewer will expect you to know how to do this.

Trainee's:
IA's are often the first thing a trainee is expected to learn. Often when starting the job the university will do an "intensive week" of 5 days, designed to allow you to learn and conduct a full IA by the end of the week. During this week you will do many role plays of these assessments. Starting with the individual segments and ending in a full 45 minute roleplay.
At the end of the module, you will either be assessed by doing a recorded roleplay (OSCE) or by being recorded doing a full assessment with a patient. For both of these you will be asked to write a reflective essay on your performance.

*For this guide I have put in a basic script on how to introduce each section. This is a guide only and the university may ask you to consider how to word each section based on more current guidelines. Also consider your own style when developing these and how you would actually naturally speak. To aid this I have added the key points in **bold**.*

Also to be noted, this guide is based on the university best practice guide. You may see other PWP's in service, adapt or even omit parts based on service protocol (or therapist drift from best practice).

What is an IA?:
- An IA is designed to find out more about what symptoms the patient is presenting with.
- It helps choose the best treatment plan best for the patients presenting problem.
- It helps assess barriers for treatment or anything that excludes the patient from treatment.
- It's semi structured: It has various sections with certain aims.
- Lasts approximately 45 minutes.
- Can be over the telephone, face to face or even by a virtual clinic.

An IA has three main sections: Information Gathering, Information Giving and Shared decision making.
The information gathering is also known as a "patient centred interview". This is designed to identify the patients main symptoms and to aid with diagnosis of the patient's main problem.

Gathering:
1) Effective questioning skills (using the **Funnelling** technique).
2) Collecting routine outcome measures **(MDS).**

Giving:
3) Clear introduction given to the patient about the assessment and its various sections.
4) Psychoeducation on diagnosis.
5) Psychoeducation on treatments available.

Shared Decision Making:
1. Problem-Statement.
2. Setting goals.
3. Deciding on a treatment plan.

When put together, the order of an assessment looks like this:

1. Introduction
2. Main Problem
3. Main Impact
4. Risk
5. Routine Outcome Measures/Minimum Data Set (MDS):
6. Additional Information
7. Problem Statement
8. Goals And Barriers
9. Provisional Diagnosis And Treatment Options.

Trainee Tip: This guide will go into each section. It will be useful to read this prior to your "Intensive Week" to give you a good basis to learn from. After your intensive week, you should know all this information rather well. But it can be useful to read over it a few times to aid your understanding of each section before your first real IA with a patient.

*The next few sections outline all the steps of an IA in detail. It is **not** recommended for the interview stage. It will be an information overload which is not required to get the job. Give it a brief read, but feel* **no need to learn or memorise it.**

IA Introduction:

Purpose: The introduction section is designed to provide the patient with some understanding of what the IA is for, and inform them of what is about to occur. For many patients this can be their first time reaching out for mental health support. This can be daunting, and having a good introduction can go a long way in making them feel more comfortable.

A good introduction should include:
1. Ensuring you are talking to the right person and asking their **preferred name**.
2. Introduce your **own name**.
3. Inform them of your **job title** and that you work as a part of a wider team.

4. Set the **agenda** you will be going through; including:
   - Main problem.
   - Impact.
   - Risk and safety.
   - Questionnaires (mds).
   - Additional information.
   - Goals.
   - Discussing the treatment plan.

🍎 *Trainee Tip: you want to do this in as little time as possible. When doing an OSCE or recording for your assessments you will be on a time limit. Also patients get bored easily. Aim for maybe 2 minutes at the max.*

Example Introduction Script:
*"To start, Can I just confirm your **full name**? Do you have a **preferred name**? **My name** is [Name] and I am a **Trainee Psychological Wellbeing Practitioner**. This means I have **specific training** in common mental health problems such as anxiety and depression. I work as a part of a **wider team** of specialists who may also be involved in your care later on.*

Agenda: *Today we are going to do an initial assessment to come to a **shared understanding** of the **main problem** you are experiencing and how this might be affecting you. The first part of the assessment includes **discussing your symptoms.** We will focus on how you have been feeling physically, how your behaviours have changed and any thoughts you may be having. And how they have been **impacting your life.** Then we will discuss any **risks around safety** you may be experiencing such as suicidal thoughts. We will then go through some **questionnaires** about your symptoms. After this we will then set some **goals for therapy and discuss treatment options.** This should last approximately **45 minutes.** [For telephone IAs: During the assessment I will be **making notes** so if you hear me typing or going quiet for a second that will be why]. As we only have 45 minutes I **may have to interrupt** you at times to bring the focus back to fit everything in. Do you have any questions about what we are going to do?"*

Confidentially:

Purpose: This section is to inform the patients about the limit of confidentiality. This is an important topic that will get covered on the course and within your service in more detail. Throughout the job there will come a time when you will be duty bound to break confidentiality. The patient knowing this is a possibility prior to the disclosure makes that conversation much less stressful for yourself. This statement is a part of the introduction section.

Example risk introduction Script:
*"This is a confidential service so everything you tell me will be kept between myself and the team here, as well as your GP where relevant. The only time this **confidentiality can be broken** is if we believe you are a **significant risk** to yourself or others, or if you disclose any potential risk to children. Then I may be duty bound to disclose this to the relevant services to get you and them any additional support required. If this was to occur it will always be done with your knowledge."*

Main Problem:

Purpose: The aim of this section is to gather information relating to the patients main problem. This information will be used as the basis of your diagnosis and lay the groundwork for selecting the best treatment.

There is no script for this section but there is an effective technique called **funnelling** you will learn and be marked against on the course. This is an important skill to use as it will be used during every IA during your career. During this section you will gather symptoms in three main areas. These areas relate to the ABC cycle. See the chapter in module two for more detail on this model.

ABC Model:
The A stands for the **autonomic** symptoms which means our physical sensations. The B stands for our **behaviours** and our actions. The C stands for the **cognitions** which are our thoughts, beliefs or images our mind produces.

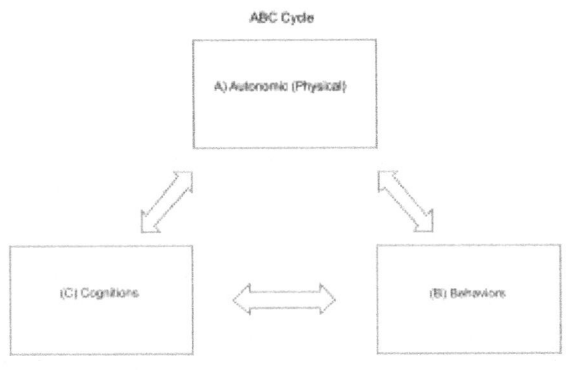

Figure 2: ABC Model

Common **Autonomic** symptoms can include:

- Low Mood
- Lack Of Motivation
- Weight Changes
- Sleeping Difficulties
- Eating Difficulties

- Increased Heart Rate
- Sweating
- Increased Breathing
- Struggling To Concentrate
- Fatigue Or Tiredness

Common **Behaviours** can include:

- Not Doing Hobbies Or Pleasurable Activities
- Avoiding Situations
- Socially Withdrawing
- Struggling To Get Out Of Bed

- Procrastination
- Chronic Rumination
- Worrying (Counts As A Behaviour)
- Overplanning
- Reassurance Seeking
- Over Thinking

- Over Researching
- Checking
- Not Delegating

- Always Keeping Busy Or Using Distraction
- Avoidance

Common **Cognitions** can include:

- "What's The Point"
- "Things Won't Get Any Better"
- "It's All My Fault"
- "I Worry All The Time"
- "I Can't Stop Worrying"
- "What If's" Catastrophic Thinking: Eg. "What If My Partner Get Hits By A Car; What If I Get Fired"

- Making Negative Predictions About The Future – Worse Case Scenarios.
- "I'll Go Mad"
- "I Can't Control My Thoughts"
- "Worry Helps Me Plan/Prepare."
- "I Am A Failure/Bad"
- "Nothing Ever Works Out"

You will need to find out a mixture of all of these during assessments.

Funnelling:

Funnelling is an effective questioning technique which you will be required to use during your IA's. You will be highly marked on your ability to use funnelling.

Funnelling starts with asking **general open** questions first. Then the questions become more **specific** until you are asking **closed questions**. Once you reach the end of the funnel, you either clarify the information and ask more questions or you start a new funnel on a new bit of information.

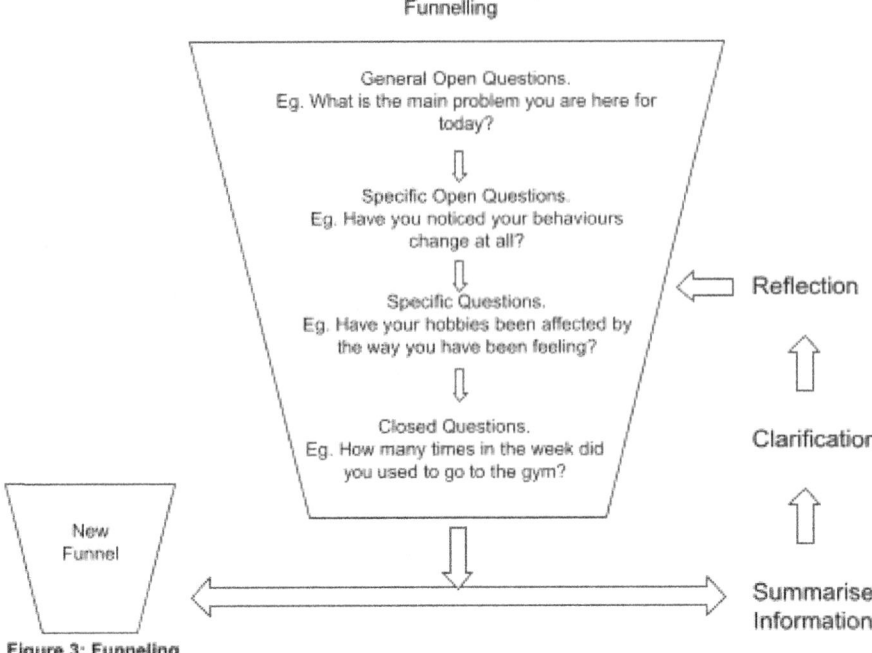

Figure 3: Funneling

General Open Questions:

Open questions are designed to allow the interview to start where the patient wishes to focus on rather than directing the patient to start on any particular area.

Examples:
- What problems are you experiencing that have led you to seek help?
- What is your main difficulty at the moment?
- What has brought you here today?

Specific Open Questions:

Specific Open questions are designed to slightly direct the interview to a particular area that the patient introduced from the last question. This prompts the patient to continue to talk about the area they themselves have chosen in more detail.

Examples:
- Have you noticed any changes in your behaviour?
- Have you started thinking differently since this has started?
- Have you noticed you get any physical sensations when you are low/anxious?
- What type of impact have these difficulties had on your life?

Specific Questions:

Specific Questions are designed to focus the interview into the specifics brought up from the previous questions. This should be related to what the patient has already discussed.

Examples:

- Have these difficulties had any impact on your hobbies?
- Tell you more about what happens when you notice you start to worry?
- Can you give me any recent examples of this?

Closed Questions:
Closed questions are designed to find out for information about a particular bit of information the patient has mentioned

Examples:
- How many hours are you sleeping?
- Where does this problem occur the most?
- Do you feel any better when around anyone in particular?

Summarise Information:
It is useful to briefly summarise the information you have heard. This provides clarification and allows you to ask more open, focused or closed questions where necessary.

New Funnel:
Once you have found out enough about the particular bit of information you have been funnelling. It can be a good idea to open up a new funnel based on what the patient mentioned previously regarding a different symptom. You should start from a specific open question at this point. For example *"earlier you mentioned you were also having sleeping difficulties, can you tell me more about these difficulties?"*

Avoid "Double barreled questions": These are questions which contain multiple questions. This can limit the answer. For example "Have you noticed any places where you feel better or worse?". Often questions like these can prompt answers for one side of the question but can cause the patient to forget to answer the other side. This limits the quality of the information gathered. Separate the questions into "Are there any places you feel better?" and then ask "Are there any places you feel worse?".

Avoid the question "Why?": It often has a negative connotation. See the difference between "So why are you worrying so much" vs "what do you think is causing you to worry more?". Ban the use of the word "why".

Using this funnelling method you should gather the A's, B's and C's as mentioned at the start of this section.

After this stage you should have a pretty good idea of what diagnosis the patient has. If not, maybe do some more funnelling (you may have missed something important), or bring the case to your supervisor to discuss in your weekly supervision meetings.

End section with a small summary. **Dont outline every symptom** you have gathered but use a small summary as this will show the patient you have heard and understood them.

Main Impact:

Purpose: This section is designed to find out if the patients functioning as changed in 5 key areas:

1. Work: One of the aims of IAPT is to get people back into work. Work can contribute to the patients main problem, be a trigger or even be where they feel better. Understanding more about this is important.
2. Hobbies: This often gets impacted by depression. Depressed patients often struggle to do many activities that they find enjoyable. Pay extra attention to asking about this with that patient group. It's also an important consideration for treatment. See chapter on treatments and "Behavioural Activation".
3. Relationships: This can often be a trigger for people or can act as a good motivational tool for setting goals.
4. Social: This gets impacted in most of the disorders. Withdrawing from people is common in depression. Or can be a symptom of avoidance for anxiety.
5. Home management: This is most often impacted by depression but can also be seen for anxiety disorders due to avoidance.

Example script on how to introduce this section:
"We are now going to discuss how this problem has been impacting your life. We will discuss in more detail how you have been affected in relation to your work, relationships, home and social life."

As usual it is best to end this section with a small summary.

🍎 *Trainee Tip: Often you may find out a lot of information about the 5 areas from during the main problem section. Rather than asking again it can be good to reflect what they have previously said and then ask if there are any additional areas of impact.*

Example: "You have already mentioned you are struggling with your home management as you feel tasks are piling up. Are you finding anything else hard in regards to managing at home?"

Risk Assessment:

Purpose: This section is to assess the safety of the patient throughout treatment.

A risk assessment will be performed during every IA and treatment session with patients. The exact specifics of the assessment can be different based on your service. Much clinical judgement is made during any risk assessment.

Example script on how to introduce this section:
*"This section will go through questions about **risk and safety**. Some of these questions may be relevant to you and some may not be. The aim is to ensure **you and others around you** remain safe during treatment and to ensure you get the best treatment possible. We will go through this at **every appointment** as risk can change over time."*

*During the university course a **full risk assessment** needs to be demonstrated. During an OSCE or recording, you can immediately fail the whole assessment for not completing this section adequately or missing questions out.*

Ask a question/s for each of the following:

Current Sucide Risk:
- *Suicidal Thoughts:* e.g. Are you currently having any thoughts about ending your own life?
- *Suicidal Plans:* e.g. Do you have plans to currently end your life?
- *Suicidal Actions:* e.g. Are you taking any actions currently towards ending your own life? (eg. stockpiling medication).

Past Sucide Risk:
- *Suicidal Thoughts:* e.g. Have you ever had any thoughts about ending your own life?
- *Suicidal Plans:* e.g. Have you ever made any plans to end your life?
- *Suicidal Actions:* e.g.Have you ever done anything towards ending your own life in the past?

Current Self Harm:
- *Self Harm Thoughts:* e.g. Are you currently having any thoughts about harming yourself in any way?
- *Self Harm Plans:* e.g. Do you have plans to currently harm yourself?
- *Self Harm Actions:* e.g. Are you taking any steps towards harming yourself at the moment?

Past Self Harm:
- *Self Harm Thoughts*: e.g. Have you ever had thoughts about self harming in the past?
- *Self Harm Plans*: e.g. Have you ever planned to self harm in the past?
- *Self Harm Actions:* e.g. Have you ever self harmed before?

- *Risk From Others*: e.g. Do you feel in danger from anyone at the moment in any way?; or "Do you feel scared of anyone at the moment?"
- *Risk To Others*: e.g. Do you think you could be a danger to anyone at the moment in any way?

- *Self Neglect:* e.g. Are you currently looking after all your basic needs at the moment (such as eating and washing)?
- *Risk To Any Dependants: e.g:* Do you have any one who relies on you for care? How is your ability to look after their needs at the moment?

Intent:
- *Likelihood of acting on suicidal thoughts from 0-10:* eg. What would the likelihood of you acting on any thoughts or plans of ending your own life be at the moment from 0-10.

Ensure the patient understands this question is about short term likelihood. If not, some patients will score more than zero "just because they can never rule it out".

Helpline Numbers:
- During the risk assessment you also need to provide helpline numbers for out of hours support. Usually to the Samaritans and an NHS crisis team for your local area.

Suicide Safety Plan:
- Should the patient display a moderate risk to self but still something which can be managed within your service you may discuss a safety plan with the patient. This plan can change from service to service. A good plan should have practical steps the patient can do as an alternative to ending their life. This should include ways to manage their emotions (distraction, activities) and as well someone close to talk to (add phone numbers of friends and family members). It should also include speaking to their GP and using crisis numbers should they feel they can not keep themselves safe.

The three factors which determine sucide is when a person views there situation as:
- *Intolerable:* The patient views their pain and suffering as truly awful. They simply can not tolerate this feeling. eg. *"I just can't cope any longer"*
- *Inescapable:* The patient can not see any way out of this feeling. eg. *"I have tried everything and nothing helps me feel better"*
- *Interminable* (endless): The patient can not see an end from the pain and suffering and believe it is never going to stop. eg. *"I will always feel depressed, nothing I do can ever change that"*.

A good safety plan should therefore help the patient realise at least one of these is not true:
- That their pain is not **intolerable** and there are things they can do when feeling like this to reduce the feeling and get through it. *Get them to think about what they did in the past when they felt this way and how they coped.*
- That their pain is not **inescapable** and there are things they can do when feeling like this to reduce the feeling. *Get the patient to think of fun activities or distractions.*
- Get the patient to realise they don't feel this way all the time. The pain is not **Interminable** (endless). Is it context or situation dependent? *Get them to see it isn't always going to be this way.* They can write something like this in their risk plan: *"I am feeling this way now, but it usually only lasts a week then I feel better"*.

End this section with a small summary of what was discussed just like any other.

Interview tip: Having a small knowledge of risk is needed for the interview. It is okay if you have never managed risk in a previous job before. They don't expect you to be an expert. But be prepared to answer questions about what you would do if a patient displayed risk.

A good answer should include:

1. *Assess the risk:*
   - *Using questions such as above. A great answer would include looking at both current as past risk. As past risk can indicate current risk.*
2. *Alerting and discussing risk with others if needed:*
   - *Discuss the case with your supervisor or the person responsible for risk within your service.*
   - *Balancing confidentiality and when breaking it is necessary.*
3. *Manage the risk if a patient can keep self safe:*
   - *Offer Helpline numbers.*
   - *Actively review this at every meeting.*
   - *Risk management plan.*
4. *Manage the risk if a patient can not keep themselves safe:*

Immediate Risk : Should the patient be in any current danger of acting immediately you can break confidentiality to call the emergency services or any next of kin.

Less Immediate Risk:

Should the patient be able to keep themselves for at least a few hours, then calling the local crisis or secondary care services is advised and they will contact the patient. This should be a priority referral.

Should the patient not be able to guarantee their safety throughout treatment but is not going to act right now. This type of risk is often too high for IAPT usually and should go to a crisis or a secondary care team who can manage risk. Usually less urgent referral.

Trainee Tips:

- *Ask risk questions directly without being hesitant. Patients can be shy of answering these types of questions should the therapist seem less confident.*
- *Use your judgement on how in-depth you go. If something feels wrong or the patient is hesitating before answering then maybe do some more exploring.*
- *Pay attention to question 9 on the PHQ-9 questionnaire used in the next section to see if it matches up with the risk assessment.*
- *Should a patient not want to answer any of these questions. Explore why. Does the patient feel it is not relevant; have they had bad experiences of opening up to someone in the past; do they think they might "get locked up". Normalise and overcome these barriers. Inform them this is a psychological assessment and that assessing their risk and safety is important for ensuring the best treatment plan.*

Routine Outcome Measures/Minimum Data Set (MDS):

Purpose: This section is designed to assess the level of the symptoms the patient is experiencing using a set of questionnaires.

The **Minimum Data Set** or as it is simply called the " **MDS**" is a set of questionnaires collected during IAs and treatment sessions. Collecting this data is central to evaluating the effectiveness of treatment and IAPT. These help assess the severity of the patient's symptoms, give a metric to assess if the therapy is working.

Example script on how to introduce this section:
*This next section is about **assessing what severity of symptoms you have been experiencing**. To achieve this we will go through some **standard questions from a questionnaire**. We will go over these questionnaires at every appointment to assess how these change throughout treatment. This allows us to know if the therapy is working or if we need to change approaches."*

There are 4 main MDS's used:

1) **Patient Health Questionnaire 9** - Known as the PHQ-9:
The PHQ-9 is not a screening tool but helps monitor the severity of depression and response to treatment. It is a self report questionnaire. Patients are asked to fill this out based on the average of the last two weeks and to select the score which best represents them.

PHQ- 9

Over the last 2 weeks, how often have you been bothered by any of the following problems?	Not at all	Several days	More than half the days	Nearly every day
1 Little interest or pleasure in doing things	0	1	2	3
2 Feeling down, depressed, or hopeless	0	1	2	3
3 Trouble falling or staying asleep, or sleeping too much	0	1	2	3
4 Feeling tired or having little energy	0	1	2	3
5 Poor appetite or overeating	0	1	2	3
6 Feeling bad about yourself — or that you are a failure or have let yourself or your family down	0	1	2	3
7 Trouble concentrating on things, such as reading the newspaper or watching television	0	1	2	3
8 Moving or speaking so slowly that other people could have noticed? Or the opposite — being so fidgety or restless that you have been moving around a lot more than usual	0	1	2	3
9 Thoughts that you would be better off dead or of hurting yourself in some way	0	1	2	3
	PHQ9 total score			

The score for each question is added up to a total score.
Depression Severity:
- 0-4 none,
- 5-9 mild,
- 10-14 moderate,
- 15-19 moderately severe,

- 20-27 severe

IAPT Caseness:10   *see section bellow for what this means
Max score 29

🍎 *Trainee Tips: This scale (and the GAD-7) is based on how "bothered" the patient is by a symptom, not the presence of the symptom. This is an important distinction to inform the patient. Forgetting this can lead to scores being much higher than they should be.*

2) **General Anxiety Disorder 7** - known as the GAD-7:

The GAD-7 is administered the same way as the PHQ-9.
The GAD-7 is not a screening tool but helps monitor the severity of generalised anxiety and response to treatment.

GAD-7

Over the <u>last 2 weeks</u>, how often have you been bothered by any of the following problems?	Not at all	Several days	More than half the days	Nearly every day
1 Feeling nervous, anxious or on edge	0	1	2	3
2 Not being able to stop or control worrying	0	1	2	3
3 Worrying too much about different things	0	1	2	3
4 Trouble relaxing	0	1	2	3
5 Being so restless that it is hard to sit still	0	1	2	3
6 Becoming easily annoyed or irritable	0	1	2	3
7 Feeling afraid as if something awful might happen	0	1	2	3
GAD7 total score				

The score for each question is added together for the total score.
Anxiety Severity:
- 0-4 none,
- 5-9 mild,
- 11-15 moderate,
- 16-21 moderately severe

IAPT Caseness: 8
Max score: 21

3) **Work and Social Adjustment Scale** - Known as the "WASAS" (pronounced: WAS-AS).

This questionnaire is designed to look at the functioning of the patients and where this impact is the most.
The areas assessed at the same as in the main impact section
1. Work
2. Home Management
3. Social Activities:

4. Private leisure activities
5. Family and Relationships

Each area is assessed from 0-8. Zero being no impact. And 8 meaning very severe impact.

Work and Social Adjustment

People's problems sometimes affect their ability to do certain day-to-day tasks in their lives. To rate your problems look at each section and determine on the scale provided how much your problem impairs your ability to carry out the activity.

1. **WORK** - if you are retired or choose not to have a job for reasons unrelated to your problem, please tick N/A (not applicable)

0	1	2	3	4	5	6	7	8	N/A
Not at all		Slightly		Definitely		Markedly	Very severely, I cannot work		☐

2. **HOME MANAGEMENT** – Cleaning, tidying, shopping, cooking, looking after home/children, paying bills etc

0	1	2	3	4	5	6	7	8
Not at all		Slightly		Definitely		Markedly	Very severely	

3. **SOCIAL LEISURE ACTIVITIES** - With other people, e.g. parties, pubs, outings, entertaining etc.

0	1	2	3	4	5	6	7	8
Not at all		Slightly		Definitely		Markedly	Very severely	

4. **PRIVATE LEISURE ACTIVITIES** – Done alone, e.g. reading, gardening, sewing, hobbies, walking etc.

0	1	2	3	4	5	6	7	8
Not at all		Slightly		Definitely		Markedly	Very severely	

5. **FAMILY AND RELATIONSHIPS** – Form and maintain close relationships with others including the people that I live with

0	1	2	3	4	5	6	7	8
Not at all		Slightly		Definitely		Markedly	Very severely	

W&SAS total score

All numbers are added together to give a max score.
Max score: 40
- 0-10 show subclinical impact
- 10-20 indicate significant functional impairment
- 20-40 indicate moderate to severe impact

The max score is rarely used. Any particular area showing above an 4 indicates clinically relevant impact in that one area.

4) **IAPT Phobia Scale:** *This scale is being dropped from the mandatory list of routine outcome measures but some services may still want this collected for its clinical significance.*

This questionnaire is designed to assess for avoidance for phobias, agoraphobia or social anxiety.

The max score for each area is an 8. Anything above a 4 shows significant avoidance

IAPT Phobia Scales

Choose a number from the scale below to show how much you would avoid each of the situations or objects listed below. Then write the number in the box opposite the situation.

0	1	2	3	4	5	6	7	8
Would not avoid it		Slightly avoid it		Definitely avoid it		Markedly avoid it		Always avoid it

Social situations due to a fear of being embarrassed or making a fool of myself [ ]

Certain situations because of a fear of having a panic attack or other distressing symptoms (such as loss of bladder control, vomiting or dizziness) [ ]

Certain situations because of a fear of particular objects or activities (such as animals, heights, seeing blood, being in confined spaces, driving or flying). [ ]

General MDS Tips:

Caseness:

The PHQ-9 and GAD-7 have a number called "Caseness". This refers to when (or not) the patient's symptoms are clinically relevant. Anything above the caseness score is known as "above Caseness" and anything below is "Below caseness".

- The aim of treatment is to get a patient from above caseness into full recovery (below caseness). If successful then the patient's recovery is recorded as a success.
- Typically if a patient is below caseness when they enter the service, they may benefit from watchful waiting rather than treatment.

Once the patient has done the questionnaires; reflect the scores back to the patient and ask if the patient agrees with the scores and feels they are accurate.

As with any section; end with a small summary and ask if the patient has any questions.

Trainee Tips:

- *Many patients (and PWP's) dislike doing these questionnaires as they can feel repetitive. Reinforce the rationale with patients on why these are useful to assess if treatment is working.*
- *These can be good guides on severity. But high scores in isolation is not a rationale to step the patient up to high intensity CBT.*
- *Many services are introducing the ability for patients to fill out the MDS online prior to sessions. Still reflect these back at the patient as if you would if they had done them in session.*
- *Online MDSs can occasionally lead to a patient who scores under caseness despite all the symptoms gathered during the IA. If this is the case it is best to review the questionnaires again. Patients can misunderstand how to fill these out or be in a rush and just answer without thinking. Failing to do so can lead to the patient not receiving the required treatment.*
- *There is no need to memorise the individual questions on the MDS. I have administered 1000s of these and even I still can't remember them. Memorising the cut off scores for caseness is recommended though.*

Interview Tips:

- *Interviewees are not expected to know what the MDS's are or how to administer one.*
- *Dropping in the names of these will make you sound very knowledgeable in the interview.*
- *Mentioning any previous experience of administering psychometric tests is advised.*

Additional Information:

Purpose: This section is designed to find out more about the patient's previous history of mental health, past treatments, and to find out if there are any barriers to treatment at this time.

Example script on how to introduce this section:
*"Now we are going to go over some **lifestyle and health questions** to help inform **what treatment is most suitable** and if their are any **barriers** to treatment at this time"*

This section will change based on the service you work for. Additional information can usually be broken down into a few sections.

Mental Health:

- Previous Episodes.
- Previous Treatment.
- Any other Current Treatment.

These questions are designed to find out more about the patient's history. Long standing or recurrent episodes may be rational for a step up. It is also important to know if the patient has had therapy before. If a patient has tried step 2 treatment multiple times before, it may be rationale for a step up.

Finding out if the patient is currently receiving any other mental health support is recommended. Only one form of therapy is recommended at a time as they can conflict. It is also good to know if the patient is under any other NHS teams that may require a joint up care (eg. perinatal support or long covid or other long term conditions). Finding out what therapy has worked in the past is also advised.

Substances:

- Prescribed Medication.
- Herbal/Over the counter medications.
- Alcohol.
- Drugs.
- Caffeine.

These questions help inform you about the patient's lifestyle. Current medication and concordance to it is an important factor to know about. Asking about herbal or over the counter medications can help uncover any safety behaviours (discussed later in this chapter for anxiety disorders).

Drugs and alcohol use can be barriers to engagement. Often services have exclusion criteria around this.

Caffeine is linked to anxiety and is always worth exploring with patients as many are not aware of this.

Physical Health:

- Is the patient (or their partner) pregnant.
- Any neurodiversity (ADHD, Dyslexia, Autism).
- Long term Health Condition.

Physical health is important for mental health. Explore if the patient has any long term health conditions.

Most perinatal patients get prioritised for treatment so explore if the patient or their partner is expecting. It is also advised to find out if they have a young child. The perinatal period is up to 1 year post pregnancy (2 years in some services).

Being aware of neurodiversity can help with a treatment plan to make adaptations where necessary.

Problem Statement:

Purpose: This section is designed to help the patient identify their own main problem.

Once you know more about the patient's presentation and symptoms it can be useful to help the patient recognise their problems from a "CBT perspective". To help aid with this we use a tool called the "Problem Statement".

Functions of the problem statement:
- Helps the patient view their symptoms in a different way. Often patients may not be able to see how their symptoms all interact together.
- It also helps make the IA more collaborative as it includes the patient into a shared understanding rather than being told a "diagnosis".
- It provides a reference point for future treatments between yourself and the patient.
- It can be revisited at the end of therapy to see what has changed since it was created.
- It helps during supervision when discussing the case.

The problem statement is a short summary of what the patient feels is the most relevant symptoms. A good problem statement should have:
1. At least one key autonomic symptom.
2. At least one key behavioural symptom.
3. At least one key cognitive symptom.
4. Mention the main impact.
5. Mention any important triggers.

An good example using all of these could be:

My main problem is that I feel tired all the time (1). When I feel like this, I just end up lying in bed all day (2) thinking about "how I am such a failure" (3). This often gets triggered at work when I get things wrong (5) and it is impacting my ability to work and look after the home (4).

Often a problem statement might not be as well crafted as this. But as long as you follow a basic template such as the one below they should contain all the relevant information.

My **Main Problem** is:
My Main **Triggers** are:
The Main **Physical** Symptoms I have been getting are:
The ways my **Behaviours** have changed are:
My main **Thoughts** are:
The Main **Impact** all of this is having on my life is:

Example script on how to introduce this section:
*"Now we are going to move on to create what we **call a problem statement**. It is a **brief summary** of what we have discussed today and the **symptoms you are experiencing**. The problem statement is helpful to check we have a **shared understanding** of your problem. It will be in the **first person** and **I can help you structure it by starting a sentence and with you finishing it with what is most important to you.** As this is a summary of what we have discussed previously you can select your answer from what we have discussed. So don't worry if it feels like you are repeating yourself."*

End section with reading this statement back to the patient and asking if they would like to add to change anything to it.

Interview Tip:
- *This isn't required for the interview and it is highly unlikely a question around this will be asked. But be aware of the term problem statement just in case.*

Trainee Tip:
- *Practice using ABC cycles during roleplays and turning them into problem statements. Getting the statement to feel fluid can take some practice.*
- *To aid collaboration the patient can be asked if they want to write or read this statement back themselves, or if they prefer you too.*

Goals and Barriers:

Purpose: This section is designed to find out what the patient is expecting or wants out of therapy. This can help when deciding on a treatment plan. This section also explores any barriers to therapy.

Example script on how to introduce this section:
*"Now we are going to discuss what specific goal we are going **to work towards** in therapy. This goal is* **set by you** *on what you feel is* **most important for you to achieve**. *Do you have a specific goal in mind? [After the goal is set] Is there anything that could get in the way of us achieving that goal?"*

Some patients will be very good at setting goals, while others may be more vague and just want to *"be happy"*. When a goal is vague it is worth asking for more detail. For example, you could ask *"what would you do differently if you were more happy"* or *"If you were more happy, what changes would you see"*. This can turn *"be happier"* into something more concrete such as *"I would be more active and start doing things again like going to the gym"*.

When creating a goal it is often recommended to think about "SMART goals".

SMART goals is an acronym to make a goal more:
- **Specific:** *What exactly is the goal going to be?*
- **Measurable:** *How do we know if it has been completed or not?*
- **Achievable:** *Is this goal actually achievable?*
- **Relevant:** *Is this goal relevant for therapy?*
- **Time Bound:** By *when does the patient want to achieve this?*

A therapy goal doesn't need to fit all of these. But the more SMART it is the better it will be. Often a "SMART-ish" goal will suffice.

 *Trainee Tip: Do not underestimate the value in setting a good goal. Goal setting is fundamental to CBT. It will determine what treatment a patient will get. If a patient goal is not a CBT suitable goal then the patient may not benefit from sessions. A supervisor may even send you back to reassess goals after supervision should the goal set not be suitable.*

Barriers:
When exploring barriers with the patient it is advised to use the "COM-B" model. (More detail on this in our chapter on Barriers and COM-B).

Interview Tip:
- *COM-B is not required for the interview. This is a recent addition to the PWP course so if the interviewer qualified years ago then they may not know much about this themselves.*

Briefly for now. COM-B refers to the patients:

1. Capacity.
2. Opportunity.
3. Motivation.

Capacity: Does the patient have the ability to achieve their goal at this time. For example, a patient who has recently become unable to walk might not be able to achieve the goal of running a marathon next week.

Opportunity: Does the patient have the resources needed to actually achieve the goal. For example a patient who wants to start swimming. Do they have a local swimming pool?

Motivation: Does the patient currently have the motivation for change. Does the patient actually want to change? There are sometimes when patients will greatly benefit from therapy but it is just not the right time for them. Some patients will drop out of therapy. Knowing the patient's level of motivation and helping the patient stay motivated can help improve engagement and reduce the chances of dropping out. Motivation for out of session work is also key. Some patients can seem highly motivated and engaged during a session but never do any homework.

Trainee Tip:
- *COM-B is an important model to familiarise yourself with. When doing treatments it can be useful for dealing with barriers in treatment sessions.*
- *A good assessment that explores barriers can make future treatment sessions easier.*

Provincial Diagnosis And Information Giving:

Purpose: This section of the IA allows for shared decision making between yourself and the patient. It is good practice to inform the patient of what their provincial diagnosis is and provide some psychoeducation symptoms if necessary.

Following this, CBT and guided self help should be explained. Offer and explore the treatment options available. It is good practice to get the patient to do an ABC cycle (More on this in the chapter on treatments).

🍎 *Trainee Tip: During module one (unless your university does module one and two at the same time): You do not need to necessarily know the treatments in detail but know enough to inform the patient of the options. More detail in the treatment chapter. For now ensure you at least know which treatment is for what disorder. See below.*

Step 2 Treatment Options:

Depression:
Behavioural Activation (BA) or Cognitive Restructuring (CR).

Generalised Anxiety Disorder:
Worry Management; Worrytime and Problem Solving.

Agoraphobia or Specific Phobias:
Exposure and Habituation.

Panic:
Panic Management.

Example Script:
*"All our therapy options we offer are **evidence based** treatments based on **Cognitive Behavioural Therapy**, or CBT for short. Have you heard anything about CBT?*

*CBT focuses on **breaking something we call the vicious cycle**. Those experiencing symptoms of low mood/anxiety commonly experience symptoms in three areas: How we **Physically feel, Our Behaviours** and our **Thoughts**. These then **interlink and have a knock on effect with each other**, which is known as a **Vicious Cycle [explain ABC cycle]**.*

*Just to check, could you **repeat back to me your understanding of the vicious cycle** and how your current difficulties would fit into a vicious cycle?*

*CBT focuses on **breaking this cycle** by either **changing our behaviour or our thoughts**: [Give example of breaking a cycle].*

Once the patient understands the ABC cycle then you can give them a brief understanding of the treatment option/s. It is good practice to give them some materials for them to read. They can then choose the option they prefer.

Ending The IA:

Purpose: Ending the IA is very important. It can be useful to summarise the sections you covered and ask the patient if they have any questions.

This section will change in service depending on the outcome of the assessment.

Often as a trainee you will be bringing the case to your supervisor before treatment is offered. Setting up an appointment to discuss the next steps is often advised.

End an IA with a brief summary:

Example Summary: *"Just to summarise today's assessment. We have talked about the:*
- ***Main problem** you have been experiencing.*
- *Explored how this has been **impacting your life.***
- *We talked about **risk to ensure you are safe.** And **went over the numbers** you can call if you felt unsafe.*
- *We then did **some questionnaires** to assess your symptoms.*
- *We then **set goals for treatment***
- *And talked about the **type of treatment offered here.**"*

Initial Assessment Chapter Conclusion:

Hopefully this chapter has given you a good idea of what an initial assessment looks like.

Interview Stage: Don't worry overly about completely understanding the structure outlined here. It is more important for you to know about why an IA is done for the interview.
IMPORTANT: *For the role play in an interview, **only focus on the main problem and impact sections**. You are not expected to even know the sections of an IA, let alone attempt it in an interview. Maybe throw in one or two risk questions. If you can implement even a fraction of the skills mentioned you will most likely perform highly.*

Trainee Before Intensive Week: You will learn the whole process during your intensive week. Reading this in advance has hopefully given you a good framework to work from. If after reading this you don't fully understand the process. Don't worry, the intensive week is highly effective at teaching you how to perform an IA. It will all make sense shortly. Most practitioners come away from the week knowing all the basics. Reading this will provide you with a good framework going into your lectures.

Trainee After Intensive Week: You should know this section really well by now. I told you it will all make sense shortly. It will only be a few weeks till you will be required to do your first real assessment. Read through this guide on areas you feel unsure about. Role Plays can be stressful. But do as many as you can. Shadow some real assessments in your service if possible.

Diagnosis (Step 2):

PWPs do not give formal diagnoses in IAPT as we are not trained for any formal diagnosis (This guide will still use words like diagnosis etc for simplicity's sake). Despite this, you will be expected to know what disorder the patient is presenting with based on the initial assessment. For each disorder, I will give some common symptoms. For a comprehensive guide and official criteria, use the DSM-5 criteria published by the American Psychological Association (APA). It will also explore the most common symptoms to look for during an IA.

 *Interview Tip:*
You are not expected to know how to diagnose. But have a good understanding of depression and generalised anxiety disorder. Those will be the main two disorders seen most within IAPT. Show the panel you have done your research on this.

 *Trainee Tip:*
You will get better at this over time. During supervision you will be asked what disorder you think each patient has. Look for the key symptoms listed below. You can also use the MDS's to aid with this. For anxiety disorders; pay extra attention to the cognitions as this is the key factor between all of the anxiety disorders.

Depression:

Depression: is a low mood that lasts for weeks or months and affects your daily life.

Key Symptoms:
- Depressed mood
- Loss of interest or pleasure
- Significant weight gain or loss
- Insomnia or excessive sleeping
- Patient appears slow physically to others
- Fatigue
- Feelings of worthlessness, guilt or negative thoughts regarding self, the world or the future.
- Poor concentration
- Suicidal thoughts

Timeframe: Symptoms must be present for at least a 2 week period.
Impact: Must cause significant impact or distress.
Differential diagnosis: Must not be better explained by another mental disorder, substance use, and no history of mania or hypomania

Common things to look for during an IA:

Autonomic:
- Low mood
- Lack of motivation
- Weight changes
- Sleeping difficulties
- Eating difficulties

Behaviours:
- Lack of Hobbies
- Not facing responsibilities
- Putting off tasks (avoiding and/or procrastination)
- Socially withdrawing
- Struggling to get out of bed
- Self sabotage behaviours
- Chronic rumination (overthinking the past)

Cognitions:

Often depressed patients have many negative automatic thoughts (NATS) in three broad categories:

The Self:	The Future:	The World:
<ul><li>"I am ugly"</li><li>"I am worthless"</li><li>"I am a failure"</li><li>"I hurt everyone around me"</li><li>"I am incompetence"</li><li>"I am always getting things wrong"</li><li>"I hate my life"</li><li>"It's all my fault"</li></ul>	<ul><li>"Things will always be this way"</li><li>"I will fail"</li><li>"Things can only get worse"</li><li>"I won't get better"</li><li>"Nothing ever goes well"</li><li>"People will leave me</li></ul>	<ul><li>"No one loves me"</li><li>"Everyone hates me"</li><li>"No one values me"</li><li>"People just put up with me"</li><li>"No one respects me"</li><li>"The world is terrible"</li></ul>

 *Trainee Tip:*

Two main areas are important when selecting a treatment option:

1. *Check the patient's activity levels, especially if the patient mentions they feel less motivated: The main impact section of an IA is usually good for identifying things the patient has stopped doing. Should they be doing less pleasurable activities, or avoiding their responsibilities then behavioural activation (BA) is a good treatment plan. More on this in the next module.*
2. *Check the patient's cognitions for any negative automatic thoughts (NATS). Some patients can struggle to identify cognitions. Asking questions relating to concrete examples can aid with this. Eg. "What were you thinking about when your friend didn't respond to your text". Should a patient have a lot of negative thinking then cognitive restructuring (CR) would be a good treatment option.More on this in the next module.*

MDS used in IAPT: PHQ-9

Anxiety Disorders:

Most of the anxiety disorders have overlapping or identical autonomic and behaviours. Cognitions will be the key in getting the correct diagnosis.

These are the main anxiety disorders seen in IAPT:
- Generalised Anxiety Disorder (GAD).
- Panic Disorder.
- Agoraphobia.
- Specific Phobia.
- Obsessive Compulsive Disorder (OCD).
- Social Anxiety.
- Health Anxiety.
- Post Traumatic Stress Disorder (PTSD).

Generalised Anxiety Disorder (GAD):

Generalised anxiety disorder is where you feel anxious most of the time. Symptoms of generalised anxiety disorder vary from person to person, but include constant worrying, a sense of dread and difficulty concentrating. This is the most common anxiety disorder you will see in IAPT.

Key Symptoms:
- Excessive anxiety and worry in a range of situations, events or activities.
- Worrying is difficult to control or not engage in.
- Feeling nervous, anxious or on edge
- Fatigue
- Poor concentration
- Irritability
- Increased muscle tension
- Difficulty sleeping

Timeframe: Symptoms must be present for at least 6 months.
Impact: Must cause significant impact or distress.
Differential diagnosis: Must not be better explained by another mental disorder, or substance use

Common things to look for during an IA:

Autonomic:

- Edginess or restlessness
- Fatigue
- Impaired concentration or feeling as though the mind goes blank
- Irritability
- Increased muscle tension
- Difficulty sleeping
- Weight changes
- Eating difficulties

Behaviours:

- Excessive worrying
- Overplanning
- Reassurance seeking
- Over-thinking
- Over researching
- Checking
- Not delegating
- Always keeping busy or using distraction
- Avoidance

Cognitions:

Lots of worries starting with "What if.."

- "What if I can not pay next month's bills?"
- "What if I lose my job?"
- "What if I mess up at work?"
- "What if I miss the deadline?"
- "What if I don't get a parking spot?"
- "What if there is traffic and I am late?"
- "What if my son/daughter/loved one gets hurt?"
- "What if my partner leaves me?"
- "What if I make my children anxious?"
- "What if my health declines?"

Always thinking the worst in situations:

- "It will go wrong"
- "What if it rains"
- "What if I fail the exam"

Thoughts about needing to always be in control.

- "I live my life by a planner"
- "I always need a plan"
- "Things have to go right"
- "I need to be in control"
- "I always need to know what is going to happen"

Might view problems as difficult, hard or overly stressful:

- "I worry all the time".
- "I can't stop worrying".
- "I cant cope when things go wrong"
- "I would be so stressed"
- "No one will be able to help"

Positive Beliefs about the value of worrying:

- "Worrying helps me find solutions"
- "Worrying helps me stay motivated"
- "Worrying prepares me for the worst"
- "Worrying helps me avoid bad things"
- "Worrying prevents bad things from occurring"
- "Worrying shows I care"
- "Worrying helps me understand my problems"

Beliefs about the dangers of worry:

- "I'll go mad"
- "I can't control my thoughts"

Trainee Tip: GAD is often easy to spot.

1. *Patients will have a lot of "what if?" worries. Ask them to tell you even the small worries they have.*
2. *They often always assume something bad is going to happen.*
3. *They may say they have always been "a worrier"/anxious.*
4. *Very important: find out how long they spend worrying a day.*
5. *Find out if they worry about things within their control or also over things they can not influence. Eg. Paying a monthly bill vs a random car crashing.*
6. *Sometimes less aware patients will say they have "free floating" anxiety or just feel anxious but not know why. Try to get them to think about any worries they have had today. Or look for what triggers their anxiety and ask questions about the trigger.*
7. *Positive beliefs about worrying can indicate a step up may be required.*

MDS used in IAPT: GAD-7

Panic Disorder:

Is a mental health condition where you have regular panic attacks. The dangerousness of the symptoms or the panc itself is over-inflated and the patient can fear the symptoms or future panic attacks.

Key Symptoms:
- Recurrent panic attacks that cause intense fear, which peak within minutes.
- Persistent worry about a panic attack occurring
- Maladaptive changes in behaviour due to panic attacks (such as avoidance or safety behaviours)

Timeframe: Panic attacks must be recurrent and frequent. For at least a month following a panic attack, patients have maladaptive changes in behaviour or thinking due to the presence of panic attacks.
Impact: Must cause significant impact or distress.
Differential diagnosis: Must not be better explained by another mental disorder, substance use or medical conditions.

Common things to look for during an IA:

Autonomic:

Typical physical symptoms of anxiety based on the fight or flight response:

- Shortness of breath
- Palpitations
- Chest pain
- Lump in throat/difficulty swallowing
- Skin losing colour
- Numbness
- Sweating
- Heartburn

- Stomach difficulties
- Shaking
- Dry mouth
- Racing thought
- Distorted vision
- Jaw pain
- Muscle pain
- Headaches

B:

- Overplanning.
- Reassurance seeking.
- Always keeping busy or using distractions.
- Avoidance.
- Safety behaviours.
- Breathing techniques.

Cognitions:

Thoughts about the physical symptoms:

- "I thought my heart was going to stop"
- "I won't be able to breathe"
- "I thought I was dying"
- "I am going to collapse"
- "I am going to have a heart attack"

Thoughts of how scary panic attacks are or fear of another episode:

- "It felt awful"
- "The panic keeps happening"
- "I won't be able to cope"
- "I am going to panic"
- "I am going to lose control"
- "No one can help me"
- "What if i die"

- "I am going crazy"
- "I need to get out"
- What if i have more panic attacks"

Patients can often have mental images that occur during or about the panic attack:

- Imagining themselves passed out
- Imagining being rushed to hospital
- Imagining there death

Trainee Tip:
1. *Find out what they think is happening for each of their physical symptoms. The patient will often see them as harmful in some way. Eg. "I thought my heart was going to stop"*
2. *Find out what they are catastrophising. What's their worst case scenario?*
3. *Patients can often say their panic attacks last hours or all day. This indicates they are not having a panic attack. Panic attacks are acute lasting from minutes to around 20 minutes. They may be having a lot of anxiety or stress symptoms throughout the day if they say this.*

MDS used: IAPT phobia and avoidance scale

Agoraphobia:

Agoraphobia is a fear of being in situations where escape might be difficult or that help wouldn't be available if things go wrong. This leads to avoidance of those situations.

There is a misinterpretation in popular culture that agoraphobia is a fear of being outside of one's home, or a fear of open places. Be aware this is not the definition as you will find patients who are fine with open places.

Key Symptoms:
- An extreme fear of two or more locations
- Avoidance of these feared locations
- The patient fears these situations due to thoughts that escape or help will not be available in the event of developing panic-like symptoms
- The same situation almost always provokes fear
- The fear is out of proportion to the situation

Timeframe: No specific timeframe required
Impact: Must cause significant avoidance
Differential diagnosis: Must not be better explained by another mental disorder, substance use, medical conditions or situational factors.

Common things to look for during an IA:

Autonomic:

Agoraphobia can occur with panic attacks and so has all the same symptoms:

- Shortness of breath
- Palpitations
- Chest pain
- Lump in throat/difficulty swallowing
- Skin losing colour
- Numbness
- Sweating
- Heartburn

- Stomach difficulties
- Shaking
- Dry mouth
- Racing thought
- Distorted vision
- Jaw pain
- Muscle pain
- Headaches

Behaviours:

- Avoidance
- Safety behaviours
- Overplanning
- Reassurance seeking
- Always keeping busy or using distraction
- Breathing techniques
- Ensuring easy exit; scanning for the exits or positioning close to them
- Zones of safety (patient may find certain areas "safe" such as there home)
- Dependence on others

Cognitions:

- Same cognitions as for panic disorder.

A strong emphasis on trying to avoid the panic happening:

- "I can only go out with someone was with me"
- "I watch out for any signs that something bad can happen"
- "I try to avoid busy places"
- "I need to take a calms tablet with me just incase"

A strong worry about the negative consequences of if they were to panic in public:

- "I won't be able to escape"
- "I will be ignored, no-one will help me"
- "I will never get home"
- "I will embarrass myself, and be ridiculed"
- "I will be trapped"

 *Trainee Tip:*
1. *The main difference between panic and agoraphobia is the act of avoidance.*
2. *Assess for any safety behaviours. Anything the patient does to "cope" going to their avoided place.*

MDS used: IAPT phobia and avoidance scale

Specific Phobia:

A specific phobia involves an intense, persistent fear of a specific object or situation. This is always out of proportion to the actual risk. This often leads to avoidance of the feared object or situation.

Key Symptoms:
- An extreme fear of a specific object or situation
- The same situation almost always provokes fear
- Avoidance of these feared locations or objects
- The fear is out of proportion to the situation

Timeframe: Persistent fear has maintained for at least 6 months
Impact: Must cause significant distress or impaired functioning
Differential diagnosis: Must not be better explained by another mental disorder or situational circumstance

Common things to look for during an IA:

Autonomic:
All of the typical symptoms of anxiety: Acute in the situation:

- Shortness of breath
- Palpitations
- Chest pain
- Lump in throat/difficulty swallowing
- Skin losing colour
- Numbness
- Sweating
- Heartburn
- Stomach difficulties
- Shaking
- Dry mouth
- Racing thought
- Distorted vision
- Jaw pain
- Muscle pain
- Headaches

Behaviours:
- Avoidance of phobic object/situation
- Safety behaviours
- Overplanning
- Reassurance seeking
- Using distraction
- Breathing techniques
- Dependence on others

Cognitions:
Thoughts are dependent on the feared object or situation.
- "I must get away"
- "I can't stand it"
- "I can't cope"
- "It is dangerous"
- "Something bad will happen"
- What if it bites/hurts me"

MDS used: IAPT phobia and avoidance scale.

Step 3 Disorders:

As a PWP you will not (in most cases) be treating step 3 disorders. However, you will need to know about them to be able to assess and accurately step up patients. This is also important for Depression and GAD as effectively recognising which step is required due to severity. This section will cover the most common A's, B's and C's to look for during an IA. This will not be an exhaustive list but will be a useful tool to start with when training. Don't just rely on this guide and always use case management supervision in regards to step ups, and clinical skills to expand on this knowledge.

Author Disclaimer: I am not a step 3 CBT therapist. This section is written to the best of my knowledge and current competences as a PWP.

Interview tips: Knowledge of these are not needed for the interview. No need to memorise any of this. However if you were to demonstrate a knowledge of which disorders are step 3 in an interview that would be very impressive.

Trainee Tip: You will get better at recognising these over time. Good knowledge of these is important for assessments as you can more accurately step patients up when required, rather than struggling during treatment sessions.

Depression:

Step 3 depression has the same criteria as in the step 2 section as it is not a seperate disorder. The only difference is the level of severity in the NHS stepped care approach. However, typically patients can have more rules, assumptions, core beliefs and self esteem issues.

Rules:
We all have rules in life. They are necessary to cope with everyday life. Eg. I need to turn up to work. However, in depression we can start to learn unhelpful rules we live by which cause our mood to worsen or maintain depression. Unhelpful rules tend to be unrealistic, inflexible and non adaptable.
A rather humorous way to think and spot rules is to remember the word "Must-erbation". Rules often start with "I must" or "I should".

Some examples
- "I must always look my best"
- "I must always try my hardest"
- "I must be always be funny"
- "I should always put others first"
- "I should never be lazy"

Assumptions:
Negative assumptions are where a person assumes something has to be a certain way or there will be a negative outcome.

Assumptions often have a similar pattern of "If *X* then *Y*"
Some examples
- "If I don't look my best, then people will think I am ugly".

- "If I don't try my best, then I will fail".
- "If people don't laugh at my jokes, then I must not be funny".
- "If I don't put others first, then I am a bad person".
- "If I am lazy, then people at work will dislike me".

Just the presence of rules and assumptions don't instantly make a person not suitable for step 2. Pay attention to the goals of the patient to see what they want to focus on.

Core Beliefs:

A core belief is a strong belief an individual has which often developed over a long time frame. These beliefs do not shift based on evidence that contradicts them and usually are tied to a strong emotional reaction. These beliefs usually are central to the patient's life, especially when in a low period. Often they can be in the form of "I am..", "People are.. ", and "The world is...".

Examples Include:
- "I am helpless"
- "I am unlovable"
- "I am worthless"
- "I am bad"
- "People are selfish"
- "People are dangerous"
- "The world is a terrible place"
- "The world is pointless"

Core beliefs can be difficult to challenge during step 2 CR and a step up is advised. BA can still be effective in reducing the effects of depression at step 2 but a step up is sometimes required based on if the core belief is maintaining the low mood.

Self Esteem:
Poor self esteem is common with depression. Although it is not a diagnosis in itself. Low self-esteem can act as a barrier to step 2 treatment if it is the cause or maintenance of the low mood. Low self esteem presents with rules, assumptions and core beliefs relating to how the individual perceives themselves. Mild self esteem may be a symptom of depression and may be responsive to step 2 treatment but long standing self esteem may require a step up.

Generalised Anxiety Disorder (GAD):

Step 3 GAD has the same criteria as in the step 2 section as it is not a seperate disorder. The only difference is the level of severity in the NHS stepped care approach. Typically patients will have greater intensity of anxiety and resistance to letting go of worrying. Patients may also have cognitive avoidance, negative problem orientation, strong intolerance of uncertainty and have positive beliefs regarding worry.

Cognitive Avoidance:
Patients with severe anxiety may try to avoid thinking about the things making them anxious. They will use mental distraction techniques, they may internally repeat positive phrases and reassure themselves everything is going to be fine. They may also externally use avoidance or distraction to always be busy to avoid thinking about their problems.

Negative Problem Orientation:
Patients may struggle to deal with problems. They see even small challenges as great obstacles. This either leads to avoidance or procrastination; Or leads to over-preparing and preemptively (and unnecessarily) removing all potential obstacles. Some patients can feel they can't handle problems well or they feel they wouldnt cope well if their feared situations were to occur.
Look out for phrases such as:
- "I can't tolerate or cope with all this worrying".
- "I have no control over my worries".
- "I wouldn't know what to do".

Strong Intolerance Of Uncertainty:
Some patients struggle with any uncertain situations. This can be for minor things such as being unable to try a new dish at a restaurant, to being as big as affecting them from applying for a new job. Step 2 patients will often show some level of this as well. Try to find out how much of an issue this is for the patient.

Positive Beliefs Regarding Worry:
Patients can start to believe worrying is helpful. Look out for any of the following:
- "Worrying helps me find solutions"
- "Worrying helps me stay motivated"
- "Worrying prepares me for the worst"
- "Worrying helps me avoid bad things"
- "Worrying prevents bad things from occurring"
- "Worrying shows I care"
- "Worrying helps me understand my problems"

GAD is extremely responsive to step 2 treatment. It can be worth always starting at step 2 unless the patient is showing a large amount of these additional factors.

Obsessive Compulsive Disorder (OCD):

Obsessive compulsive disorder (OCD) is a common mental health condition where a person has obsessive thoughts and compulsive behaviours. This is often paired with the patient fearing the meaning of having these thoughts and can feel they are overly responsible if their feared situation was to occur.

Key Symptoms:
- Presence of obsessions which are recurrent and persistent thoughts, urges or images. These are unwanted and cause distress
- The patient attempts to ignore, suppress or neutralise these thoughts by performing a compulsion.
- Presence of compulsions which are repetitive behaviours or mental acts which the patient feels driven to complete in response to an obsession to reduce the feelings of distress.

Timeframe: Obsessions and compulsions must be time consuming (take more than 1 hour a day)
Impact: Must cause significant distress or impaired functioning
Differential diagnosis: Must not be better explained by another mental disorder, medical condition or substances

IAPT Questionnaire used: Obsessive-Compulsive Inventory (OCI).

OCD is a disorder that is arguably one of the most commonly misunderstood disorders by the public, who often use the term when they "like things clean". If a patient mentioned they are a bit OCD, chances are they are using the term incorrectly. So be aware if a patient is using the term not to just assume they have OCD.

Obsessions/Intrusive thoughts:

A patient with OCD usually experiences frequent obsessive thoughts. These thoughts will be distressing to the patient. A patient with OCD will often place an importance on why they are having the thought. For example, a patient could have an intrusive thought about stabbing their loved one. A patient will be disburbed about why they have had such a thought. They may feel ashamed, bad or really concerned. They may even confuse having that thought with wanting to do it. Intrusive thoughts are common in the general population (it is almost guaranteed you the reader have had some, or many). But without OCD, a person will not place any importance on them, as they just think something like "that was a strange thought" and never think of it again. The patient's concern and worry about these thoughts causes them to occur more frequently which causes a vicious cycle. Obsessions can also be in the form of images or urges that repeatedly enter the mind. These cause feelings of anxiety, disgust or unease.

Obsessions are typically the last thing a patient with OCD wants to occur. That's what makes them so distressing. And mix in the belief that having that thought must say something about you as a person, leads to extreme distress.

Compulsions:

Patients will then experience some sort of compulsive behaviour in response to the intrusive thoughts. A compulsion is a repetitive behaviour or mental act that the patient feels they need to do to temporarily relieve the unpleasant feelings brought on by the obsessive thought. Almost any behaviour can become a compulsion. This can be something internal and invisible (cognitive) or external and visible (an action).

For example, someone with an obsessive fear of their house burning down, may feel they need to check that the fire alarm works several times before they can go to bed.

Obsessions can be about anything but usually follow certain themes:

1. Contamination
   - Body fluids
   - Germs
   - Diseases
   - Contaminants (radiation etc)
   - Chemicals
   - Dirt
2. Losing Control
   - Fear of acting on impulses to harm oneself, or others
   - Getting violent images or thoughts
   - Fear of saying obscenities or insults
   - Fear of stealing something
3. Harm
   - Fear of being responsible for a bad event like a fire
   - Fear of harming others for not being careful
   - Fear that you have already harmed someone and forgotten about it
   - Fear that they want, or will harm someone
4. Perfectionism:
   - Needing to know or remember things
   - Concerns over order, patterns or exactness
   - Fear of forgetting or losing something important. This can lead to hoarding compulsions
5. Unwanted sexual thoughts:
   - Taboo thoughts
   - Obsessions over sexuality
   - Obsessions involving children or incest
   - Obsessions over aggressive sexual behaviour
6. Religious:
   - Concerns over offending God/s or blasphemy
   - Concerns over morality and right and wrong
7. Relationship OCD (termed rOCD):
   - Severe concerns over being good enough for their partner. This is not related to self esteem. It can be about qualities such as morality
   - Severe concerns over if they love their partner. Thoughts about other people can disturb the patient and cause them to doubt their love
   - Severe concerns over thinking others are attractive. Often linked to the theme above
   - Severe concerns over either themself or a quality in their partner
   - Severe obsessions over a particular body part. E.g. strongly disliking the partner's nose (to an extreme degree)

Compulsions can relate to any action that reduces a patient's distress. This can often follow similar patterns. Some examples include:

1. Washing and Cleaning:
   - Excessive cleaning, showering, bathing, or other grooming routine
   - Cleaning objects
   - Preventing contamination
2. Checking:
   - Checking that nothing bad has occurred
   - Checking body parts or symptoms
   - Checking no harm was caused to self or others
   - Checking doors, ovens or other objects
   - Reassurance seeking or questioning others over checks
3. Repeating:
   - Repeating thoughts in head
   - Repeating actions or activities in an order
   - Doing things in multiples (eg. counting to 4)
4. Mental Compulsion:
   - Reviewing memory
   - Counting
   - Praying
   - Replacing words or images in head
   - Mental distraction

Social Anxiety:

Social anxiety is a strong fear of social situations that does not go away. It occurs in everyday activities, relationships and at work which relate to social situations and reduce self confidence. A patient will feel worried before, during and after these interactions.

Key Symptoms:
- Persistent fear of social or performance situations.
- The patient feels that they will act in an embarrassing or humiliating way.
- The patient recognises that their fear is unreasonable or excessive to the situation.
- Social situations are avoided or endured with intense anxiety

Timeframe: Anxiety must be persistent for 6 months
Impact: Must cause significant distress or impaired functioning with the patients normal routine, occupation, social or relationships.
Differential diagnosis: Must not be better explained by another mental disorder, medical condition or substances

IAPT Questionnaire used: Social Phobia Inventory (abbreviated as SPIN)

Common symptoms:

Autonomic:

- All the typical anxiety symptoms; Increased heart rate, sweating, creased breathing etc
- Weight changes
- Sleeping difficulties
- Eating difficulties
- Struggling to concentrate
- Fatigue or tiredness
- May feel they sweat, or blush in front of others

Trainee Tip: Try to find out what symptoms they believe others might be noticing e.g. "People can see me shaking" and what that means e.g. "people can see I am anxious and might think I am weird".

Behaviours:

- Excessive worrying about social situations
- Overplanning social events
- Reassurance seeking
- Checking
- Ruminating on past social events
- Always keeping busy or using distraction
- Avoidance

- Self-focused attention: During social situations they will focus highly on themselves or how they perceive they are coming across to others
- Not being present in social situations
- Lots of safety behaviours. Eg. Avoiding eye contact, holding objects
- Controlling the flow of conversations to "safe topics"

Trainee Tip: It can be useful to explore a recent social situation and see what the patient was focusing on (It will most likely be themselves; how they are coming across, or thinking on what to say or do next.)

Cognitions:

Cognitions will revolve around:

- How they feel they should come across in situations. Eg. "I must act confident"
- How they feel they are coming across in situations. Eg. "I look shy and I start shaking"
- How they believe others are perceiving them. Eg. "Others can see I am anxious when I shake and see me as under confident"

Some examples include:

- "Others are looking at me'
- "They think I am stupid/ugly/fat/odd"
- "They will notice I am sweating/blushing/shaking"
- "They will think negatively of me/judge me"
- "I'll be embarrassed"
- "I don't like being in the spotlight"
- After the situation: 'It was terrible, others think I am weird, I'm not good enough"

Trainee Tip: Just the presence of a patient being anxious about social situations doesn't mean social anxiety. This is an intense fear that causes impacted functioning. Often patients with GAD may worry about the odd social situation. Making differential diagnosis an important consideration (see criteria G of the DSM-5.

Health Anxiety (Illness Anxiety Disorder):

Illness Anxiety Disorder (used to be called hypochondria) is known more commonly as health anxiety in IAPT. Health Anxiety Disorder is when a patient is overly concerned they are ill, or will become ill. This usually starts to take over their life and preoccupies a lot of their time and worries.

Key Symptoms:
- Preoccupation with having or becoming seriously ill
- Physically symptoms of illness are not present, or only mild. If a medical condition is present then the preoccupation with illness must be clearly excessive
- The patient is easily alarmed regarding their health
- The patient performs health related checking, or avoidance of checking symptoms

Timeframe: Anxiety regarding health must be present for at least 6 months
Impact: Preoccupation with health leading to a high level of anxiety.
Differential diagnosis: Must not be better explained by another mental disorder, medical condition or substances

Common Symptoms:

Autonomic:

- Patients can have all the usual symptoms of anxiety.

Behaviours:

- Checking body
- Hypervigilance to any body sensations
- Body scanning
- Reassurance seeking
- Either frequent visits to medical professionals or avoiding doing so
- Requests for further medical tests when tests are negative
- Searching symptoms online and researching possible causes of symptoms
- Can also present with the avoidance of attending medical appointments or checking health

Cognitions:

Patients will have many worries about getting ill.

- "I feel more tired than usual, maybe I have leukaemia?"
- "My parents had cancer so its likely I will too"
- "I am worried about having a heart attack"
- "I am going to get ill"
- "I am going to die"
- "I am sure i have [serious illness]"

- "When my stomach aches I think is cancer"
- "What if this mole is dangerous?"
- "What if I get cancer?"
- "What if this headache is a sign of a tumour?"
- "What if the doctors missed something?"
- "It could be anxiety but I can't take the chance incase it is something"

Often these worries will be catastrophic in nature. Always the worst case scenarios.
Patients will often have a worst case scenario for what each physical symptom can mean. Eg. A headache must mean cancer.

Patients can also have some rules and assumptions:

- I must/should/have to always: eg. "I must go to the doctor every time I get a symptom"
- My doctor must/has to always/must/should: eg. "Be professional; always be 100% sure; certain"
- I must/must not: eg. "Never ignore a symptom"; "Must get this checked out"
- If X then Y: eg. If I don't get this checked out, I could die".

Trainee Tips:
- *Ask patients what they think there physical symptoms mean (eg. tumour, cancer, heart problems)*
- *Ask what they think will happen if they did have a problem eg. will modern medicine be able to cure them or not.*
- *Ask what impact they feel a diagnosis will have on their life or dignity.*

Post Traumatic Stress Disorder (PTSD):

Post-traumatic stress disorder (PTSD) is an anxiety disorder caused by very stressful, frightening or distressing events. The patient will attempt to not think about the traumatic event or anything related to it. When this fails the patient is faced with severe distress.

Trainee Tip: Not everyone who experiences a traumatic event will get PTSD. Don't just assume a patient has PTSD when they mention a traumatic event.

Key Symptoms:
- A specific traumatic trigger is present. The patient needs to have been exposed to: death, threatned death, actual or threatened serious injurgy, or actual or threatened sexual violence. This can be directly, a witness, learning a close friend or relative was exposed to trauma or indirectly by exposure to aversive details of the trauma.
- The presence of intrusion symptoms such as unwanted upsetting memories, nightmares, flashbacks, and emotional and physical reactivity to reminders of the trauma.
- Avoidance of thoughts, feelings or external reminders of the trauma
- Negative thoughts and feelings since the trauma
- Changes in trauma related arousal since the trauma

Timeframe: Symptoms must be present for at least a month
Impact: Symptoms create distress and impaired functioning
Differential diagnosis: Must not be better explained by another mental disorder, medical condition or substances

What causes PTSD:

When a stressful or traumatic event occurs, the brain wants to learn from the experience to try and learn from the experience in an attempt to try and avoid it happening again in the future. This relies on the individual thinking over the memory and processing the events. When an event is so traumatic or horrible, we often do not want to think back to it. For those with PTSD they will highly avoid the memories or anything that can trigger these memories. This creates conflict between the brain who wants to process the memory and the person who does not. This leads to the inability to process the traumatic event. When any trigger of the memory occurs the person can experience relieving symptoms and high levels of distress.

Autonomic:

- Patients can experience all the symptoms of the fight and flight response. Especially during any re-experiencing symptoms.
- Dissociation

Reliving symptoms:

- Mental Images
- Nightmares
- Flashbacks (feels like the patient is back in the traumatic event. Not just a memory)
- Emotional reactivity

- Persisting negative emotional states such as fear, horror, anger or shame

Behaviours:

- Avoidance of triggers that can remind the patient of the event.
- Cognitive avoidance: avoiding thinking about the event
- Safety behaviours
- Behavioural avoidance: avoidance with alcohol or drugs
- Detachment from others

Cognitions:

Negative beliefs about themselves:
- "I am bad"
- "I am broken"
- "I am not the same since"

Negative beliefs about others or the world:
- "People can not be trusted"
- "People only look out for themselves"
- "People are dangerous"
- "No one understands"
- "No one cares"

Self blame or blaming others for the event:
- "The crash was my fault"
- "It was my fault i got attacked"
- "I shouldn't have been out that day"
- "If only I did things differently"
- "I should have fought back"

Patients can also have a failure to remember important parts of the events.

Trainee Tip: You don't need to find out every detail about the traumatic event. It is more important to focus on how it has affected the patient. You also don't want the patient to become highly distressed or dissociate during an IA (especially a phone IA).

Perfectionism:

Perfectionism is not classed as a mental health disorder. Therefore there is no DSM-5 diagnosis. Perfectionism tends to occur within other disorders and is an extension of low self esteem. It can act as a barrier to certain treatments. For example with BA; patients may feel they need to do all their activities perfectly, so never start; or when they do the activities, they feel they didn't do them correctly or as well as they should have. It can be a barrier to CR as beliefs around performance can be very rigid and resistant to challenging. It can also be a barrier in worry management as the patient is focused on being perfect and controlling everything.

Trainee Tip: Be aware perfectionism exists. This is not taught on the course so maybe leave reading this one till you are more competent with assessments.

Below is a commonly used model for perfectionism.

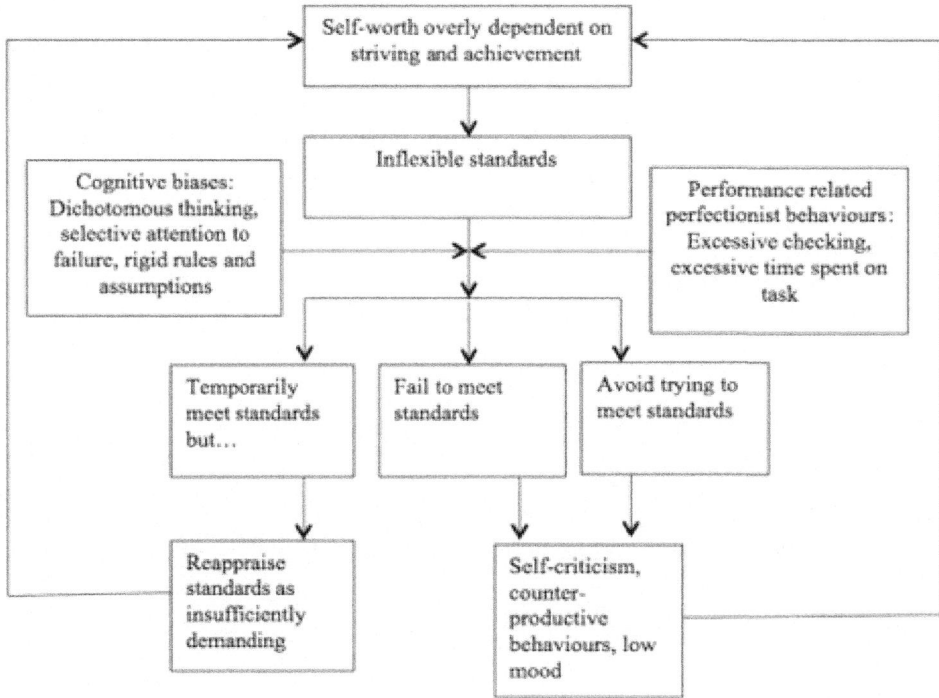

1. Self-worth is overly dependent on striving and achievement: Patients see their achievements as a reflection of themselves. If they are not achieving they can see themselves as a failure.
2. Inflexible standards: Patients will have very inflexible standards. This overlaps a lot with the rules and assumptions as stated in the step 3 depression section. A patient may say things such as "I must always get it right"
3. Cognitive biases: Patients with perfectionism will have cognitive biases such as only paying attention to when things go wrong, black and white thinking or have very strong assumptions.

4. Performance related behaviour: Patients will often do alot of behaviours to ensure that they are getting everything important to them correct. They engage in checking behaviour, or spend excessive time and resources ensuring they are meeting their standards.
5. Reappraising standards when achieving: When a patient with perfectionism does achieve they tend to up their standards. They may feel a sense of a fleeting achievement before moving on to the next task.
6. Avoiding standards: Some patients avoid trying to meet their standards as they feel it's better to not try, than try and fail. Often because if they put in the effort and fail then it proves it was their fault.
7. Self criticism: When failing to meet their standards, a patient will be highly critical of themselves.

It is worth asking a few questions about each area during an IA when perfectionism is suspected.

Diagnosis Chapter Conclusion:

Hopefully this chapter has given you a good idea of the types of mental health issues seen within IAPT and how to recognise them.

Interview Stage: As mentioned you are not expected to know fully how to recognise these disorders for the interview. However, have a good idea of depression and anxiety just in case any questions do arise.

Trainee Before Module Two: During module one you will be taught how to assess these disorders. Start getting used to recognising these as quickly as possible. Use supervision to aid with this.

Trainee After Module Two: By this module you should be treating step 2 patients. Therefore it is recommended to have a good knowledge of symptoms to help apply your knowledge in treatment sessions.

Core Competences:

Module one focuses on teaching you how to engage with patients and establish a therapeutic rapport to effectively gather information and aid the patient in collaboratively choosing a treatment programme. This will develop a set of *"Common Factor"* and *"Specific Factor"* competences to aid with this. These skills will be expanded and reinforced in each module.

Interview Tip: You will not be expected to know how to do any of these. In your interview role play they will be looking at some of these qualities. So it can be good to remember these principles but don't overly worry about them.

Common Factor Skills:

Common factor skills is a term that relates to the interpersonal communication techniques used by **any mental health professional** that are present in any effective interview. These often aid something called the therapeutic rapport/alliance. This simply means the positive relationship between the patient and therapist.

Within an IA or treatment you will use a various set of Common Factor Skills such as:

Verbal skills:

- *Empathy Statements:*

Empathy Statements are an important part of any IA or treatment. These statements are designed to improve the therapeutic alliance by making the patient feel understood and listened to. This may sound obvious but this skill takes time to learn and much practice. The idea behind these statements is that **empathy** is better than **sympathy**. Sympathy is where you have *gone through a similar experience* and try to relate to the patient based on this. Sympathy can **backfire** in therapy and reduce the therapeutic alliance if the patient feels that you don't truly understand what they are going through. Every person's experience is unique. For example, you may have been through a hellish divorce, which for you was a highly negative experience. However, a patient going through one may have a different experience. They could even be relieved. So you run the risk of not matching the patient's experience. Instead you want to use empathy instead. Empathy is where you **try to understand and acknowledge** the patient's experiences. Simply put, empathy is understanding and sympathy is sharing.

To aid this, we used something called **Empathy Statements**. These are short phrases which reflect back the patient's experience of what the patient has just said. So if a patient said that they have been "struggling with their divorce" currently; a good empathy statement could be "I can hear how much you have been struggling recently". This validates the patient and they feel understood as you are using the same terminology they are using.

The best empathy statements start by using our key senses of hearing and seeing: For example: "I can hear..." "I can see that..." "That sounds..."

It is possible to use other statements such as "That must have been quite difficult for you". However, only use these when the patient has also stated this or you run the risk of making an assumption which if incorrect, can damage the therapeutic alliance.

Trainee Tip:
During your OSCEs and recordings you will be assessed on this. Missing good empathy opportunities can cost you marks. But using them too much when unnecessary can also be bad. Practice these during roleplays. Consider recording your role plays and listen to them back while considering where opportunities for empathy statements could have been.

Interview Tip: Try throwing in just one of these in your interview role play would really set you ahead of the rest.

- *Accurate Summarising:*

During an IA it is useful to use small summaries (capsule summaries) to reflect back what you have heard. This can help clarify any misunderstandings and improve the therapeutic alliance as the patient can hear they have been understood and listened to. This is important during funnelling.

At the end of each section in the IA, it is good practice to **briefly** summarise.

Trainee Tip: Do not summarise everything. Reflect back almost as if it were in bullet form. You will be marked on your ability to summarise so do practice this skill.

- *Normalisation:*

Patients can feel that their symptoms are abnormal or that something is wrong with them for feeling the way they do. It is also not uncommon to hear patients say that their lives are good and they feel silly for feeling the way that they do. It is important to inform them that their experience and symptoms are often typical (normalise the experience). This can be with the use of statistics (eg. *one in four people at any time have a common mental health difficulty*) or by informing them there symptoms are typical or understandable (eg. *"Feeling exhausted is often a common symptom of anxiety. So you are not alone in what you are experiencing"*).

Trainee Tip: You do not need to normalise everything. It can be great to use this if the patient mentions feeling unusual in regards to any symptoms. Over-normalising can make the person feel worse. Imagine if they felt terrible and were seeking help, just for their mental health professional to repeatedly tell them it's "normal".

- *Minimal encouragers:*

These are the use of small signals that lets the patient know you are listening and understanding. Consider words like *"uh-huh"*, *"yes"*, *"no"*, *"mmm"*. This is particularly important if the assessment is over the phone.

- *Avoiding using paraphrasing:*

Do not paraphrase what the patient has said. This can cause the patient to feel misunderstood.

- *Funnelling skills:*

Funnelling is paramount. Read the section on this during the main problem of an IA.

- *Non judgmental listening:*

Patients need to feel no judgement when in an IA. If they feel judged, the therapeutic alliance can be disrupted, then the quality of the information and therapy decreases.

- *Good tone of voice:*

Consider your use of tone when talking with patients. Especially important over the phone. Adjust this to match the patient's energy. Sound engaged and interested in what the patient is saying.

Non-verbal Competences:

- *Eye contact:*

Make correct eye contact. This can help the patient feel like they are being listened to too. Be aware that too much eye contact can make patients feel uncomfortable. Adjust this for the individual patient. Eg. a patient with social anxiety may find eye contact harder. Also be aware that some cultures have different levels of comfortability around eye contact.

- *Minimal encouragers:*

Same as in the verbal section above. But consider nodding or gestures.

- *Good use of space:*

Use office space effectively. Having a large table between yourself and the patient may feel more distant.

Safeguarding tip: Always place yourself closest to the door. In the unlikely event of patient aggression you do not want them to be blocking the exit.

- *Note taking:*

Note taking is essential for the job. However, make sure you are using good verbal and no-verbal competencies and not staring at your keyboard/screen for the whole assessment.

- *Facial expressions:*

Use friendly facial expressions. If you look upset, frustrated, bored etc, the patient will notice and therapeutic rapport will suffer.

Specific Factor Skills:

Specific factors relate to the particular skills and models of therapy used by a PWP. This relates to your psychological knowledge, techniques and interventions used.

Interview Tip: You will learn all of these on the course. This guide will provide you with basic knowledge of much of this. You will not be expected to have much knowledge of how to be a PWP. Before this guide most people went into the interview with very little knowledge. Demonstrating any awareness of these will make you a very desirable candidate.

Typical specific factors skills include:

- Knowledge of how to perform an IA and its sections
- Ability to provide psychoeducation
- Knowledge of the psychological models used within step 2 (eg. ABC model)
- Knowledge of common mental health disorders
- Knowledge of how to facilitate guided self self
- Knowledge of the treatment interventions.
- Ability to make evidence based adaptations to treatments
- Ability to not drift from step 2 working.

Within an IA you will use a various set of specific factor skills such as:

- Capsule Summaries
- Larger Summaries
- Funnelling
- Psychometric testing
- Use of Problem statement

Module One Summary:

This concludes the information for chapter one.
By this point you should have as good idea regarding:
- What CBT is.
- What IAPT is.
- The role of a PWP.
- What an initial assessment is.
- How to carry out a good assessment.
- How to recognise disorders.
- A brief introduction to the core competence you need as a PWP.

Module Two: Evidence-Based Low-Intensity Treatment For Common Mental Health Disorders.

Module two is designed to teach a PWP how to deliver low intensity interventions to support patients with common mental health problems in the self-management of their own recovery.

This module will go over the evidence based treatments used within IAPT. A particular focus will be on the research base and practical processes involved in a range of cognitive behavioural self-help programmes.

This module will also expand on your common factor skills gained from module one and on adapting them for use within treatment modules.

Knowledge will be learnt through a combination of lectures, seminars, reading and independent study. These skills will be put into practice almost immediately in service and therefore have a high focus on practical skills development.

This module will be assessed with a mixture of OSCEs, essays and recordings based on conducting a full treatment session. You will also be asked to continue completing a portfolio demonstrating hours worked, and written outcomes regarding your practice. This will be supervised by your service supervisor and marked by the university.

Purpose of this chapter:
The purpose of this chapter is not to give you a full comprehensive understanding of all of the treatments used in IAPT. We will be ignoring the history and research behind these treatments. Instead we will be focusing on the rationale as used within IAPT and the basic outline of each protocol.

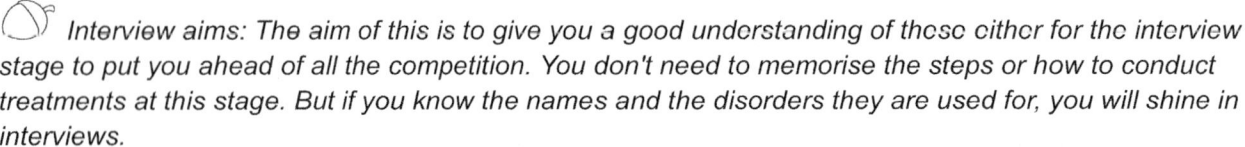 *Interview aims: The aim of this is to give you a good understanding of these either for the interview stage to put you ahead of all the competition. You don't need to memorise the steps or how to conduct treatments at this stage. But if you know the names and the disorders they are used for, you will shine in interviews.*

Trainee aims: The aim of this is to give you a good understanding of all the treatments before your university lectures to help familiarise yourself with these treatments. For my university course, only a few hours of the morning was spent on learning a single treatment, with the second half of the day spent role playing. Knowing a bit about the treatments beforehand can be an excellent advantage in getting to grips with each treatment protocol.

Note: some universities have slightly different psychoeducation points. For outcomes, essays and OSCEs use the points your university taught, as that is what they will mark you against.

What Is Guided Self Help:

A PWP delivers Low-Intensity CBT in the form of guided self help.

Guided Self Help is a structured set of sessions that revolves around a specific CBT strategy. This can be tailored to the patient's specific difficulties. The aim is to improve the patient's own understanding of their symptoms and to improve their self-management of these difficulties.

The sessions look at how the patient's difficulties operate in the 'here and now' and what may be maintaining them.

Guided self-help is recommended by the National Institute for Health and Clinical Excellence (NICE) and is a Cognitive Behavioural Therapy (CBT) based approach for supporting people with mild to moderate anxiety, and depression

Guided self help doesn't have a formal limit on the amount of sessions but 4-6 sessions is often seen as the minimum required dose. Each session is typically 30 minutes but may vary based on the case.

Guided self help requires patients to have:

- Commitment to attending sessions
- Ability to set limited achievable goals to work on during treatment
- Complete suggested reading away from sessions
- To practise the tools and techniques away from sessions

One of the key features of guided self help is the emphasis placed on the use of self help materials. The aim of a good PWP is to engage the patient with the materials as much as possible. This allows the effect of therapy to extend beyond the therapy sessions.

Treatment Structure:

Similar to an IA, treatments also have a unique structure. This structure is the same for each treatment.

1. Introduction; including self-introduction, confidentiality and agenda setting
2. Reviewing the problem statement
3. Reviewing goals
4. Medication review
5. Risk Review
6. MDS
7. Homework review
8. Session content
9. Setting homework
10. Barriers
11. Summarising session
12. Booking next session

Interview tips: You do not need to know the structure for the interview. It will be an information overload. Reading this should simply be seen as a way to increase your knowledge of a job you want to do.

Trainee aims: You will learn this structure in your module two. It can be useful to know this in advance so you can focus more on the content of the treatments in role plays rather than the structure.

Here we will break down all the sections in more detail:

1. *Introduction; including self-introduction, confidentiality and agenda setting:*

Treatment sessions should start with an introduction.
- Ensure you are speaking with the correct person
- Reintroduce yourself and your job role
- Re-Inform the patient of the limits of confidentiality

Agenda Setting: It is useful to set an agenda for the session. This can keep the session time bound and more structured.
- Outline the key steps you will be recovering (problem statement, goals, homework review ect)
- Ask the patient if there is anything they would like to add to change to the agenda.

2. *Problem Statement:*

Review the problem statement that was created during the IA. This ensures you are still working on the problem the patient has identified. It can also help with monitoring progress.

3. *Goals:*

Review the goal that was set during the IA. These goals can change between the IA and a treatment, especially if your service has a waiting list for treatment. Reviewing this can also help the patient see if improvement is occurring.

4. *Medication review:*

Briefly check if the patient has started, stopped, changed or is struggling with any medication.

5. *Risk:*

Conduct a risk assessment. This should be comprehensive. However, you can summarise your understanding from previous sessions and ask if anything has changed. Sometimes patients can open up throughout treatment and disclose thoughts or actions they didn't feel comfortable sharing during an IA.

6. *Routine Outcome Measures/MDS:*

Complete the MDS. As with an IA, reflect the scores back with the patient and review progress or deterioration.

7. Homework review:

This section is about reviewing any tasks or goals set at the last session. This can range from reading the self help materials to trying out a new strategy introduced in the last session.

Trainee Key Points:
- *Don't forget to review the patients understanding of important points from last session*
- *Find out if the patient struggled with any homework tasks, If so then explore the barriers together. See the chapter on barriers and COM-B for more information on this.*
- *Reflect on any learning the patient has from doing the tasks.*

8. Session Content:

This section is where you will go through the main intervention. See the next chapter for a detailed guide to each intervention.

Trainee Key Points:
- *Be as collaborative as possible during sessions.*
- *It is good practice to check the patient's understanding of any psychoeducation point first. They should be reading the self help materials at home (it's called guided self-help for a reason). This stops the session being you just teaching the materials. See guided self help, as you filling in gaps in the patient's knowledge rather than teaching them. Get them to read the booklet as homework.*

9. Setting Homework:

This is when homework should be set for next session

Trainee Key Points:
- *Be collaborative. Don't tell the patient what to set as homework. No one likes being told what to do, even if it's good for them.*
- *A good example of how to set homework could be "so based on what we have covered today, what do you think would be a good goal would be for you to work on between our sessions?".*
- *Should a patient struggle you can also prompt them. E.g. "So today we looked at [eg. how we use scheduling to help us overcome our low motivation]. How do you think you could apply this in your life before the next session?"*
- *It can be good to call homework "goals" or "tasks". Some patients dislike the word homework.*

10. Barriers:

After the homework is set, it is good practice to explore any barriers to achieving the homework. See the chapter on barriers and COM-B for more information on this.

11. Summarise session:

After this, do a small summary of the session and the content covered and the homework set.

12. Booking next session:

Book in the next session with the patient.

Trainee Key points:
- *Ask the patient how long they need to complete the homework.*
- *Ensure they know how to contact you if they need to change times.*

Conclusion:
Hopefully this section has given you a good idea of what an average treatment looks like.

Interview Stage: No need to understand the structure outlined here. Focus most of your efforts on the assessment skills rather than on treatments.

Trainee Before Treatment Module Starts: You will learn the whole process at the start of module two. It can be useful to know this in advance because all of the treatments have this structure. Knowing this early can make your first few roleplays much easier.

Trainee After Treatment Module Starts: You should know this section really well by now. You will be assessed on how well you keep to this structure. Practice with roleplays as much as possible. Being structured can really help when working with patients so try to stick this outline the best you can.

Treatment Information For The Interviews:

Trainee PWPs can skip to the next chapter. You might find this section useful to know as a baseline but the next section will provide more detail on each treatment and will be more relevant for module two of the course.

This guide will go into each treatment in a lot of detail. If you are applying for a PWP job you will not be required to know each treatment in any detail. Most interviewees most likely no none of them. Trying to memorise all the steps will most likely take a lot of time, and provide little benefit to your interview. It may even come at the cost of memorising other key aspects.

This section will break down the basics. If you remember just these key points you will be far ahead of any other applicant (unless they too have read this book).
The key words in bold are really good key phrases to throw into your interview.

Depression:
There are two main treatments for Depression
Behavioural Activation (Often said as the letters "**BA**" in spoken language within IAPT):

BA aims to treat depression by improving a patient's **motivation**. Patients with depression tend to **do less** and feel they can not be bothered to do anything.
This strategy aims to introduce a **balance of routine, pleasurable and necessary activities** back in their life. This is achieved by using a weekly **activity diary** to **schedule** activities.

Cognitive Restructuring (Often said as the letters "**CR**" in spoken language within IAPT):

CR aims to treat depression by helping the patient to realise the **Negative Automatic Thoughts** they are having may not be **accurate**. Patients will keep a **thought record** (a **diary** of their thoughts). They will then **gather evidence for and against** their thought being accurate. They will then come up with a **new alternative balanced thought**.

Generalised Anxiety Disorder (GAD):
The treatment for **GAD** is called **"Worry Management"**.
It has two parts:
Worry Time: Patients will select a 20m period of the day where they are allowed to worry about worries they have **no control over**. And aim to not worry outside of this worry period.
Problem Solving: Patients will aim to find **solutions** to their problems for which are within their control. They will look at all the **benefits and disadvantages** of each solution and select the best one.

Phobia or Agoraphobia:
If a patient is **avoiding** anything (phobias or a fear of any places) we use something called **graded exposure and habituation**. The patient will slowly expose themselves to their feared situations until they are no longer scared. Patients start with less feared objects/places and work up to harder ones.

Panic Disorders:
For patients who are having panic attacks we get them to realise they are not in any danger and **panic attacks are not dangerous**. This knowledge typically stops panic attacks in future. They may keep a **panic diary** to help with this learning.

Treatment Protocols:

As previously mentioned this section is aimed towards trainees. You can skip this for the interview stage.

All step 2 treatments involve *"**Psychoeducation**"*. These refer to important key points about the disorder or treatment. See these as the key points of information the patient needs to understand during treatment. The first major psychoeducation point regardless of treatment offered is the use of the ABC model.

ABC Model:

All of the treatments within IAPT revolve around the patient's symptoms and any vicious cycles the patient may be in. One of the most common ways to model this is using something called the ABC cycle (some services use the "5 Areas Model" instead, which is similar but adds two extra areas: "Situation" and "Emotion").

ABC is an acronym:
The **A** stands for the **autonomic** symptoms which means our physical sensations. The **B** stands for our **behaviours** and our actions. The **C** stands for the **cognitions** which are our thoughts, beliefs or images our mind produces.

Below is a diagram of the ABC Cycle:

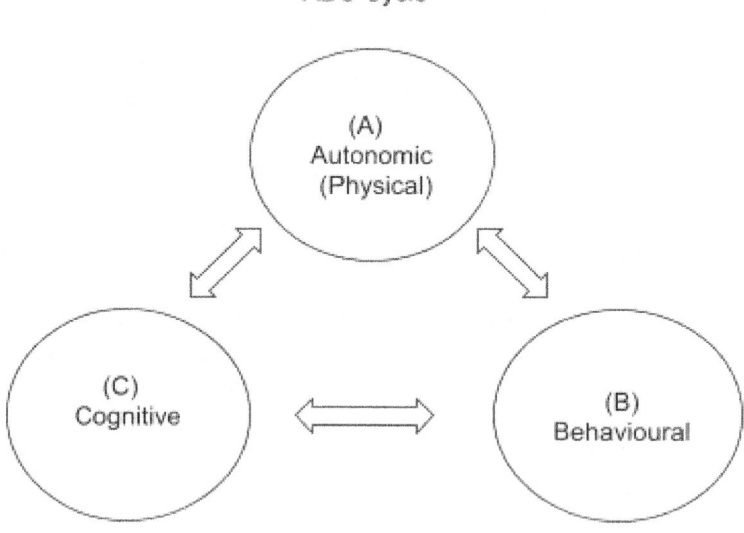

Figure 4: ABC Model

There are multi-directional arrows between each area. This symbolises how if you were to affect one area of this cycle it will have a knock on impact on the other two areas.

Let's look at four examples of this in practice starting at different areas on the model.

1) Imagine a patient who had not slept at all last night. They will be feeling physically exhausted (A), due to this they decide to rest for most of the day instead of writing an essay for university (B). They may start criticising themselves for staying up all night (C) (*"Why did I do that when I had an essay to write?" "I am going to fail now"*).

2) Imagine a patient who just got a text inviting them to a party she is dreading. *"Maybe I shouldn't go, no one likes me anyway (C)"*. So she avoids the party and doesn't go (B). But now she feels low in mood, drained (A) and lonely.

3) Imagine a patient who just made a mistake at work. *"I can't believe I just did that. I am such an idiot. Why am I always doing this? (C)"*. Because of this the patient feels low and starts to lack motivation (A). When she gets home she ends up ruminating over the mistake she made (B).

4) Imagine a patient who has stopped doing many activities (B). They sit around all day doing very little (B) and their house has become a mess. They might start to feel low and exhausted despite doing very little (A). They may end up criticising themselves (*"I am useless. I can't even keep my house tidy"(C)*.

As you can see. When a trigger happens. The ABC gets activated and something will occur in all three areas regardless of which one starts first. This can often cause a vicious cycle which maintains poor mental health. Each area has the ability to cause the others to deteriorate or improve.

This model is the backbone of the treatments with patients. It is often the first thing taught regardless of the treatment used. It is good practice to get patients to understand their own cycles throughout treatment. This will help patients become more aware of their own symptoms and how they relate to each other.

Depression:

The first step in any treatment is providing psychoeducation of the ABC cycle and what maintains depression. See the two diagrams below:

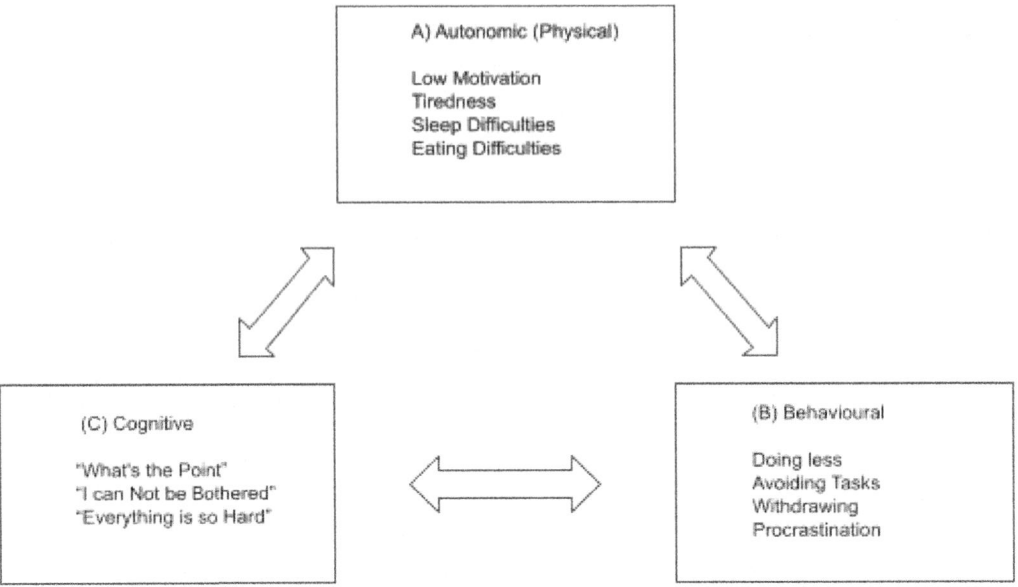

Figure 5: Example ABC Model for Depression

Below is the maintenance cycle for depression.

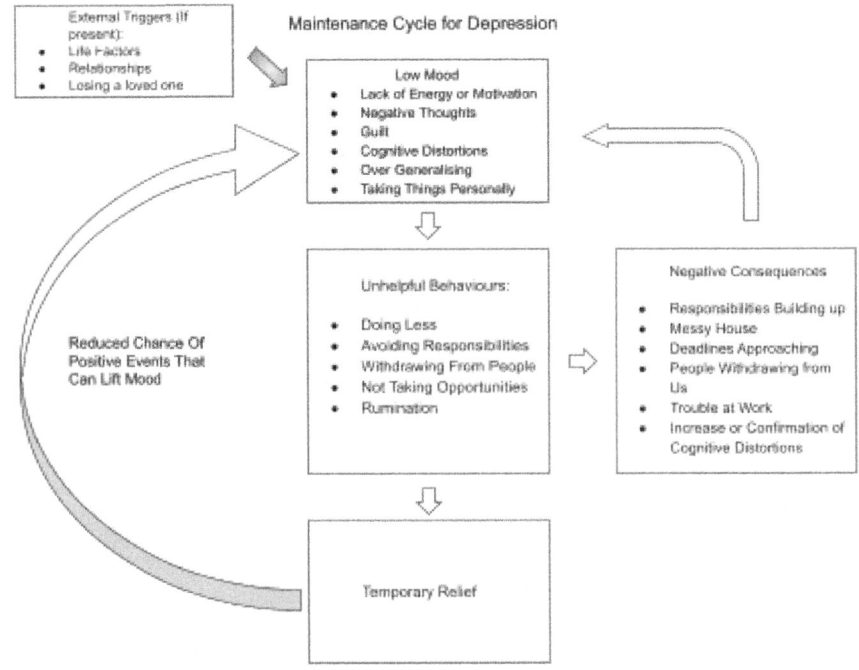

Figure 6: Example Maintenance Cycle for Depression

As we can see from the ABC and maintenance cycles for depression. Depression is originally caused by a trigger. This causes low mood, which then causes us to feel less motivated. When this happens, we do a lot of unhelpful behaviours such as putting things off and doing less. This can cause a lot of negative consequences in the patient's life which can then further act as a trigger for the patient's low mood. These unhelpful behaviours are often done in an attempt to avoid things perceived as difficult, hide from negative thoughts or feelings, or due to simply lacking any motivation or energy to do anything. This often creates a temporary sense of relief. But this in turn creates less motivation and lower mood as the patient has less chance of any positive events to lift their mood. This cycle reinforces itself and can be difficult for patients to naturally escape from. This can maintain the cycle even if the trigger has been resolved.

Often patients can often become self critical (C) about their lack of achievements due avoiding (B) all their responsibilities. The negative consequences can also affect their quality of life which itself can cause negative thoughts about their situation. Both of these in the long term can lead to cognitive distortions and negative thinking, which can maintain depression.

Based on this maintenance cycle, there are two main ways based on CBT we can treat depression

1) Increasing activity levels and reducing avoidance (and when the patient feels better, they are less likely to have negative cognitions). For this we used a strategy called Behavioural Activation (BA).
2) Tackling the cognitive distortions and negative thoughts caused by low mood (and when these subside, patients are more likely to increase activity levels naturally). For this we used a strategy called Cognitive Restructuring (CR).
3) There is a third method in some rare cases called problem solving. Should a patient's low mood be maintained by an external trigger such as debt or a fixable life event. Then problem solving to remove this trigger can also be effective to raise mood. For the university course though it is recommended to only focus on BA and CR unless your university says differently.

Behavioural Activation (BA):

Behavioural activation is a very simple but highly effective strategy aimed to improve the patients activity levels. It consists of psychoeducation around the rationale for BA + 5 main steps.

Psychoeducation:

1. ABC Cycle
2. Maintenance cycle
3. Rationale for BA including the role of motivation and how it can be created, and how activity scheduling works.

Main Steps:
0) Baseline Activity Monitoring (optional).
1) Create a list of routine, pleasurable and necessary activities.
2) Create a hierarchy (Rank how difficult these activities are).
3) Activity scheduling (Plan in when these activities will take place).
4) Do the activities.
5) Review your progress.

Psychoeducation:
Provide information on the ABC cycle and get the patient to fit themselves into their own cycle.
Explore the maintenance formulation which was in the previous section. See if the patient feels this is relevant to them.
Next outline the role of lack of motivation in maintaining low mood and how we can improve it using behavioural activation.

Step 0: Baseline Activity Monitoring (optional):

Some PWP's use baseline activity monitoring as the first step of treatment.
The aim of this is to find out a bit more about what the patient is already achieving in terms of activity, and can sometimes help see if the patient is doing too much or has an imbalance of activities in their life (see step 1).

There are various schools of thought on the pro's and con's of doing this. Most PWP's omit this step due to time constraints within sessions and the amount of sessions offered at step 2. Assuming a good initial assessment was done and good psychoeducation around the ABC cycle before BA began, then you should have a good idea about the patient's baseline activity anyway.

Step 1: Create a list of routine, pleasurable and necessary activities:

Patients are taught that there are three main types of activities.
The Routine:
This refers to activities that the patient used to do regularly. Often this can be in the form of cooking, cleaning, personal hygiene, exercise or shopping. Regular meal times or sleep hygiene can also be discussed here as these can help regulate the body to the time of day and can improve wellbeing.

The Pleasurable:
These activities are the things the patient used to enjoy before they became depressed. You can also consider things the patient would like to start doing or always wanted to try.

The Necessary:
These activities are often highly important for the functioning of the patient. They are tasks that if not done, will cause a significant negative consequence. Examples of these include, paying bills, taking medication, turning up to work, or looking after children.

Trainee Tip: Three legged stool metaphor. Get the patient to think of these three types of activities as the legs on a stool. Ask them what they think would happen if one of the legs is smaller than the other. It would fall over or not be very stable. The same applies when having an imbalance of activities in life. Imagine the stereotype of a person who spends all day on his PC gaming and watching TV. Although they are doing pleasurable activities, they are missing out on doing their routine and necessary activities and may feel depressed. Alternatively, imagine a single mother who has three young kids and is working full time. She may be managing with all the routine and necessary items but never makes any time for herself. She is also at risk for depression. The idea is to get a balance between the three activity types. Then ask the patient if they think any of their "stool legs" (types of activities) in their life are out of balance.

Trainee Tip: Routine: Focus on getting the patient a good routine in terms of eating and sleeping. These will anchor the patient. If a patient isn't eating or sleeping well then it's hard to treat depression. Imagine the impact a lack of sleep routine would have on yourself without depression.

The patient's first homework task can be to fill out a list of activities for these categories.

Here is an example of what this could look like once the patient has filled it in.

Routine	Pleasurable	Necessary
Hoover Cook three meals a day Clean the house Do the laundry Walk the dog	Read a book Paint a picture Listen to music Go bowling Meet up with my brother Learn something new Go to the gym	Pay my credit card bill Take my kids to school Do the food shopping Go to work on time Take my medication

Step 2: Create a hierarchy (Rank how difficult these activities are):

The next step after the patient has completed their list of activities is to rank them by how difficult it is to achieve. Easy, medium or difficult. It is important to remind the patient this is on how hard **they will personally** find the task to achieve given their **motivation** rather than how the general population would find it. The reason for this is that patients need to start on what they find easy.

Trainee Tip: Personal Trainer Metaphor: Just as a personal trainer wouldn't ask a first time gym member to run a marathon on day one, a therapist can expect a depressed patient to tackle their Mount Everest (hardest activities) straight away. If a patient sets the goal too high and fails they may feel worse. The only exception to this is when a really important necessary activity has an imminent deadline.

Breaking down tasks:

Another important discussion to have with the patient at this stage is on how to break down tasks into smaller and more manageable chunks. This often makes difficult activities much easier. A common example of this I see in practice is when a patient has put on their list they need to clean the house. I don't know about you personally, but even on a good day I would struggle to clean my whole house. It sounds obvious to break things down and only clean one section at a time. But when a patient is depressed their problem solving skills can be diminished (see the section on problem solving); and patients can often attempt to over achieve when planning in and underachieve in practice. Having *"clean the cupboards in the bedroom"* on their list rather than *"clean the house"* can make all the difference in a patient following through or looking at a large task and becoming demoralised.

The patient should ideally have a good mixture of routine, pleasurable and necessary in each difficulty category.

This task can be set as a homework task:

Here is an example using the last list:

	Task
Hard	<ul><li>Cook dinner (R)</li><li>Go bowling (P)</li><li>Meet up with my brother (P)</li><li>Do the food shopping (N)</li><li>Take my medication (N)</li></ul>
Medium	<ul><li>Hoover the kitchen and living room (R)</li><li>Make lunch (R)</li><li>Clean my bedroom (R)</li><li>Do the laundry (R)</li><li>Paint a picture (P)</li><li>Learn something new on youtube (P)</li><li>Pay my credit card bill (N)</li><li>Take my kids to school (N)</li><li>Go to work on time (N)</li></ul>
Easy	<ul><li>Hoover the bedroom (R)</li><li>Make breakfast (R)</li><li>Clean the kitchen counter (R)</li><li>Walk the dog (R)</li><li>Read a book (P)</li><li>Listen to music (P)</li><li>Go to the gym (P)</li></ul>

As some of the observant may have noticed, some of the activities have been broken down into easier tasks. Some tasks on here could be broken down even further. Have a think about how you could break these down further.

🍎 *Something to note here: Did you notice there are some necessary items such as taking medication that were in the difficult category? It is important to take note of these highly important tasks and help the patient break these down and figure out how to achieve these early on.*

Step 3: Activity scheduling (Plan in when these activities will take place):

The next stage is to get the patient to plan in when they are going to do some of the activities.

Rationale for activity scheduling:
When feeling low and lacking motivation it can be very hard to start doing activities. Often we can intend to start but following through is hard. Think back on a time when you wanted to start a new diet or exercise program; it was probably easier to plan to start than follow through. ***We can overcome this lack of motivation by planning our activities in.***

Start slowly with just a few easy ones and build up each week.

Follow the plan, not the feeling: Discuss with the patient the importance of following the plan rather than how they feel on the day.

Use effective planning in strategies: Planning in more detail increases the likelihood of the patient following through.

Using smart goals with planning works very well:
Specific: Plan the activity in a very detailed and specific fashion. Consider the four W's when planning in: What, When, Where and Who
Measurable: The patient needs to know when they have actually achieved their goal.
Achievable: Start with the easy category
Relevant: Use a mixture of routine, necessary and pleasurable.
Timebound: There is no point planning most things for a long time away. Plan in for the week where possible.

For example, which of these two plans do you think is more likely to be followed through on?

1) Next week I will make sure I go to the gym

2) Next Tuesday at 10am, I will go to my local gym with my best friend Tom for at least 60 minutes.

Most would argue that number two is better. It's very specific, measurable, achievable, relevant and timebound.

Example schedule:

Day	Morning	Afternoon	Evening
Monday	Put my medication and a bottle of water on my desk so I remember to take it (N)	Read at least 10 pages of a book (P)	
Tuesday		Hoover the living room for 10 minutes at 4pm (R)	
Wednesday	Make breakfast (R)		
Thursday			
Friday			Hoover the bedroom (R)
Saturday			
Sunday		Listen to music (P)	
Consider these when planning in: What, When, Where and Who.			

🍎 *Trainee Tip: Get the patient to think about how they can make each task easier to achieve. As you can see from the chart above, to help achieve the goal of taking medication, the patient has taken some practical steps to make it easier.*

Some of the plans above use SMART goals and some do not. Think for a few minutes on how you would improve on these goals?

Step 4: Do the activities:

The next step is for the patient to go away and do the activities they have planned.
Reinforce the idea of "**Follow the plan not the feeling**". Following through is entirely up to your patient to complete. If they have any issues then use the troubleshooting guide on the following pages to re-engage the patient.

5) Review your progress:

During sessions it can be helpful to review if the activities are having an impact on mood. Ideally the patient has realised they feel better after doing activities. It can also be useful for the patient to start reflecting on their progress after tasks. Some activities will increase mood more than others. They can learn to promote the ones that do and reduce the ones that have little impact.

🍎 *Troubleshooting BA:*

The patient feels they can not relate to BA:
- First stage is to ask the patient what is making them think that.
- Explore an ABC cycle with the patient. Review the maintenance cycle in detail and see if they fit into it.
- Maybe they were assessed incorrectly. Find out more about their goals and presentation.

BA seems to basic:
- Patients can sometimes see BA as too basic. Often their expectations of therapy have been moulded by TV or society, and they believe they must look into a deeper reason why they are depressed. Reinforce that BA is highly effective. Explore recent events in their life when they did an engaging activity that improved their mood. Use that as an example to show how BA already works for them; they just need to continue.
- Remind the patient that sometimes a simple effective solution is better than a complicated one. Get them to imagine if it was a physical health issue. They would always want a less intrusive and easier solution, so why not the same for mental health. eg. Not many people would choose to take 20 different medications when they could just take 1, assuming equal effectiveness.

"I do this already":
- If a patient is doing a lot of necessary and routine things they may feel they are already highly activated. Explore their hobbies and pleasurable activities. Remember the three legged stool metaphor.
- Explore the patient's cognitions. If there is another factor causing the depression then focusing on the behaviours may be less effective. For example, if the patient had a recent bereavement maintaining the depression then BA might not be as effective.
- Have you considered looking for perfectionism or low self esteem?

"My life is already run by a diary":
- Reinforce that BA is about a balance of activities.
- Reinforce that BA is a short term intervention. They won't need to keep a diary forever.
- Explore if having a diary has had any advantages for them already. If it has helped them in other areas, why wouldn't it also help with their mood.
- It is possible to do BA without activity scheduling. It's less effective but it is possible if the patient is motivated and follows the principle of BA.

"I am too busy":
- Check if it's the right time for therapy. CBT requires a time commitment for homework. Reinforce that it will only work if they make time for it. Use a metaphor about dieting: *"Even if you find the best diet plan, if you don't have time to follow it, will it be effective?"*
- Explore how much time the depression wastes for the patient. If they spend most of the day ruminating or low. Ask them if making time now, will actually create more time later.
- Explore motivation for change.

Not doing homework:
- Explore motivation for change.
- Reinforce that it will only work if they make time for it.
- COM-B.
- Check if it's the right time for therapy.

Too depressed to do homework:
- Reinforce the rationale.
- Explore with the patient the benefit of trying vs doing nothing.
- Check if it's the right time for therapy. Sometimes people are not ready for change regardless of the current impact.

"Activities don't make me feel better":
- Reinforce that this isnt always the goal. Cleaning the house may not cause a mood boost. But it can stop a mood decrease which would have been caused by a messy house.
- This may not be true. It could be a depressed thought. Get the patient to guess from 0-100 how much they will enjoy an activity before doing it. Then re-rate after they have done it.
- Reinforce that the goal is more long term than one or two activities. Keep trying and eventually you will.
- Check in with what activity they are doing. Was it stimulating enough or too hard?

Balance is off:
- Patients often do well in at least one of the three activity types (eg. too many routine activities). Try to get them a balance of the three activity types if possible.

External barriers: Eg. "It rained so I didn't do it":
- The patient is thinking too rigidly about the diary. It's a tool to improve activity, not to blindly follow.
- Get the patient to think about alternatives. We can not control the external factors (eg. rain). But we can do something different.

Self critical thoughts such as "I didn't do enough":
- Get the patient to realise that depression looks for any reason to take away the positives. They most likely did enough but can not see it due to the low mood.
- Get the patient to plan goals in a way that they know when they have achieved their goal. Set this as a low goal, and everything after is a bonus. For example, instead of "doing the dishes", say "I will wash the dishes for at least 5 minutes".

Engaging in BA but no improvement:
- Ask the patient if they have any ideas on why they may not be improving. They may have an idea.
- Is there an external factor maintaining the depression? (eg. no amount of BA is going to make you feel good if you just lost your whole family, dog, job and have just been made homeless, all in the space of a week).
- Focus on what has improved.
- Do another ABC cycle to see what is occurring.
- Step up if needed. Bring to supervision.

Cognitive Restructuring (CR):

Going back to the main rationale for what maintains depression:

Low mood causes us to feel **less motivated**. When this happens, we do a lot of **unhelpful behaviours** such as putting things off and **doing less**. This in turn **creates less motivation** and lower mood. This cycle reinforces itself and can be difficult for patients to naturally escape from.

Patients can often become **self critical** (C) about their lack of achievements due **avoiding** (B) all their responsibilities or about triggering situations in their life. This in the long term can lead to **cognitive distortions** and **negative thinking**, which can maintain depression.

As mentioned before, the second way to tackle depression is by looking at the cognitive distortions and negative thoughts caused by low mood (and when these subside, patients are more likely to increase activity levels naturally). For this we used a strategy called **Cognitive Restructuring** (CR).

Main steps in CR treatment:

1. Psychoeducation
2. Identifying Unhelpful Thoughts
3. Gather Evidence
4. Creating New Balanced Thinking

Step 1: Psychoeducation:
- Discuss with the patient if thoughts are accurate representations of the world. The answer is **they are not**. Using metaphors and thought experiments can be useful for this.
  Example metaphor:
Ask the patient if they like or are scared of dogs. Whatever their answer is, ask them to imagine walking down the street with someone who is the opposite. A dog comes walking towards the two of you. One of you will be scared and have thoughts such as *"the dog will bite me"* and one will be thinking *"aww what a cute dog"*. Both people are seeing the same dog but having completely different experiences. This should demonstrate well that thoughts really can influence how we perceive the world.
This then can be linked to depression and that when we are feeling low we have a tendency to see the worst or misinterpret the world in a negative way.
- We can change the way we are **thinking**. This can then change our **emotions**.
- Negative Automatic Thoughts (NATS): One of the main psychoeducation points is what a **NAT** is. As the name suggests these are Negative thoughts which occur **automatically** and almost instantly when a trigger occurs. An example of this is a patient who slightly raises their voice at their child and instantly thinks *"I am a terrible parent"*.
- **Hot Thoughts**: This is a term used later during treatment to describe the NAT that is most **highly linked to the negative emotion** the patient experiences. We often have many thoughts around a situation or topic. The Hot Thought allows us to focus and challenge the one causing the main impact without having to challenge every single thought the patient has.

Step 2: Identifying Unhelpful Thoughts:

The first step in CR is to get the patient to be able to recognise their own thoughts. NATS can be so automatic they can be **hard to recognise**. This is because we often feel the impact of your thoughts and just instantly believe what they are saying is true.

To help with this the patient is recommended to keep a **thought diary** in which they record the:
1. Situation prior to the NAT: This helps the patient see their triggers.
2. Thoughts: This helps them learn to recognise their NATS.
3. Belief in thought (0-100%): This is used later to see if challenging helps reduce this.
4. Emotion felt: This helps the patient see a link between their thoughts and feelings. It also helps identify the Hot Thought.
5. Intensity of Emotion (0-100%): This is used later to see if challenging helps reduce this.

Here is an example thought record:

Situation	Thoughts + Belief in thoughts (0-100%)	Emotion (Sad, guilty, anxious, angry etc) + Intensity of Emotion (0-100%)
I had a stressful day. Then my daughter wouldn't eat her peas. I snapped and raised my voice telling her to eat them or she wouldn't get dessert.	I am a bad mother (70%) I am the worst (50%) I shouldn't have done that (80%) I am always getting snappy (90%)	Sad (70%) Guilty (80%) Angry (60%)

Once the patient has filled out the chart they need to select the "**Hot Thought**". The best way to do this is look at what the highest emotion was and see which thought was most likely linked to it. In this patient's example the patient's strongest emotion was guilt at 80%. As you can see many of her NATS could be related to this. Ask the patient what they think is the most related thought. In this case it was *"I am a bad mother"*.

Step 3: Gather evidence:
The next stage is to look for evidence that supports the negative thought. And then evidence against it.

Some patients can really struggle with this section. It is important to set up a few rules for what counts as evidence. **Using bad evidence can make the patient feel worse.**

Trainee Tip: Courtroom metaphor: Get the patient to imagine they are a Judge. A defendant was accused of stealing from a shop. His evidence was "it wasnt me". Would you say that was good evidence? The patient will usually say no. Ask why. Then remind them this is similar to when they are listening to their NATS, not to use this type of weak evidence. Eg. "I am terrible: Just because I feel I am".

Get the patient to only use evidence that would stand up in a courtroom. Not based on feelings or opinion but facts.

Example of evidence for and against the thought "I am a bad mother":

Evidence for NAT:	Evident against NAT:
I did raise my voice	Most parents raise their voice at some point
I have been more snappy recently	I was only snappy that day because I as so stressed after taking my kids out for the whole day for a surprise outing to disneyland and I just needed a break after being on my feet all day
I have not been perfect recently	Nobody is perfect
	My partner always praises me for how much of a good mum he thinks I am.

You can also get patients to tear down their evidence for their NAT by asking themselves a few simple questions such as:

- Is your evidence for this based on facts or on how you feel?
- Is this a realistic thought to have?
- Could you be misinterpreting the evidence in any way?
- Are you having this thought based on facts or is it a habit?
- Are you seeing the big picture?
- Are you looking at all the evidence or just what supports your negative view?
- Are you exaggerating the evidence in any way?
- Would your best friend agree with your interpretation?
- Would this still be true if the same situation happened to someone else?
- Did someone else make you believe this thought? Are they reliable?
- Is the situation more complicated than you are viewing it?

Trainee Tip: I would also recommend for trainees to have a list like this during sessions to better help them challenge evidence for when they have a session with a particularly hard patient who really believes their NATS.

*Trainee Tip: CR is **not** about challenging the patients NATS for them. If the patient can not challenge themselves during a session, how are they going to achieve this out of the session. You can ask these questions above to help in a session but it is always best to get the patient to try and challenge their own thoughts independently.*

Step 4: Creating New Balanced Thinking:

After looking at the evidence, the patient can re-rate their belief in their original NAT and intensity of emotion at this point. Once the patient has gone through all their evidence they should be feeling slightly better and their belief rating should be lower than when it started.

If not that is an indication that:
- The patient has not gathered enough evidence against their NAT
- The patient has used bad evidence to support their NAT
- There is always the possibility their negative thought is accurate (rare)
- The patient's thought may be a **core belief** and may need a step up.

This isn't to say a patient will go from 100% belief to 0%. You may only see a 10% drop. But that's still an improvement. Get the patient to realise that if they dropped it 10% today, what's to stop that from dropping another 10% next time, and the time after.

Now the patient can create a new **more balanced thought** to replace their NAT.
This step isn't about thinking positively, it's about a **believable** and **accurate** new belief set in **reality and based on evidence.**

Based on the example we looked at:

"I am a bad mother" and be replaced with *"I am not a bad mother. Occasionally, even good mothers shout at their children when really stressed".*

Get the patient to rate how much they believe the new thought. If they don't, it's most likely just a thought based on positive thinking rather than evidence.

Trainee Tip: A new thought can be created by taking evidence from both sections of the CR chart and merging them (evidence for and against).

Full Chart Example: All the charts previously are just sections from a bigger chart. A fully completed one should look similar to this.

Situation	• I had a stressful day. Then my daughter wouldn't eat her peas. I snapped and raised my voice telling her to eat them or she wouldn't get dessert.
Thoughts + Belief in thoughts (0-100%)	• I am a bad mother (70%) • I am the worst (50%) • I shouldn't have done that (80%) • I am always getting snappy (90%)
Emotion (Sad, guilty, anxious, angry etc) + Intensity of Emotion (0-100%)	• Sad (70%) • Guilty (60%) • Angry (80%)
Evidence for NAT	• I did raise my voice. • I have been more snappy recently. • I have not been perfect recently
Evident against NAT	• Most parents raise their voice at some point. • I was only snappy that day because I was so stressed after taking my kids out for the whole day for a surprise outing to Disneyland and I just needed a break after being on my feet all

	day.
	• Nobody is perfect.
	• My partner always praises me for how much of a good mum he thinks I am.
Revised Thought + Belief (0-100%)	• I am not a bad mother. Occasionally even good mothers shout at their children when really stressed. (70%)
Revised Emotion + (intensity 0-100%	• Happy (60%)

Troubleshooting CR:

No Improvement in symptoms:

- Explore with the patient how they are doing the chart:
- They may be doing it wrong. Look through an example together.
- They may not be using good evidence. Look through an example together. Check if they are using thoughts rather than facts.
- They are not challenging the "Hot Thought". Explore this with the patient. In some cases they may need to reframe their NAT they are challenging.
- They are not giving it the attention it requires. Explore barriers to completing this and motivation with the patient.
- The patient may have core beliefs.

Core Beliefs:

A core belief is a strong belief an individual can have which has often developed for a patient over a long time frame. These beliefs **do not shift based on evidence** that contradicts them and usually are tied to a strong emotional reaction.
Imagine if the patient in the example we looked at had a core belief that "only bad parents shout at their children". It would be unlikely that going through the CR chart would change her belief. At the end she may have simply stated that even though all the evidence points against it *"I am still a bad mother for shouting"*
There is no list of what a core belief is. Almost any belief can be a core belief depending on the patient. It is often advised to look for these during the assessment stage before step two treatment starts. Screen for these in treatment when a patient is struggling to find evidence or simply can not come up with an alternative thought.

The patient is struggling to find their NATS:

- Reinforce the use of the thought diary. It can take practice.
- Get the patient to notice their emotional or physical feelings first. Use physical feelings or

  emotions as a radar for NATS. *Metaphor: Where there is smoke (emotions), there is usually fire (NATS). Use the thought record as usual.*

- Practice, practice, practice.

Generalised Anxiety Disorder (GAD):

GAD is the most common disorder you will treat within IAPT and the one for which you will probably see the highest recovery rate and lowest need for stepping up.

It has a very structured treatment protocol called Worry Management.

Steps:
1. Psycho-education on abc cycle and maintenance of anxiety.
2. Worry distinction: hypothetical and practical.
3. Worry awareness training (worry diary).
4. Worry time.
5. Refocusing skills.
6. Problem solving.

Step 1: Psychoeducation:

The psychoeducation for anxiety can be very detailed. I will go into a lot more detail here than I will recommend informing all patients off.

ABC Cycle:
Always start with an ABC cycle as usual.

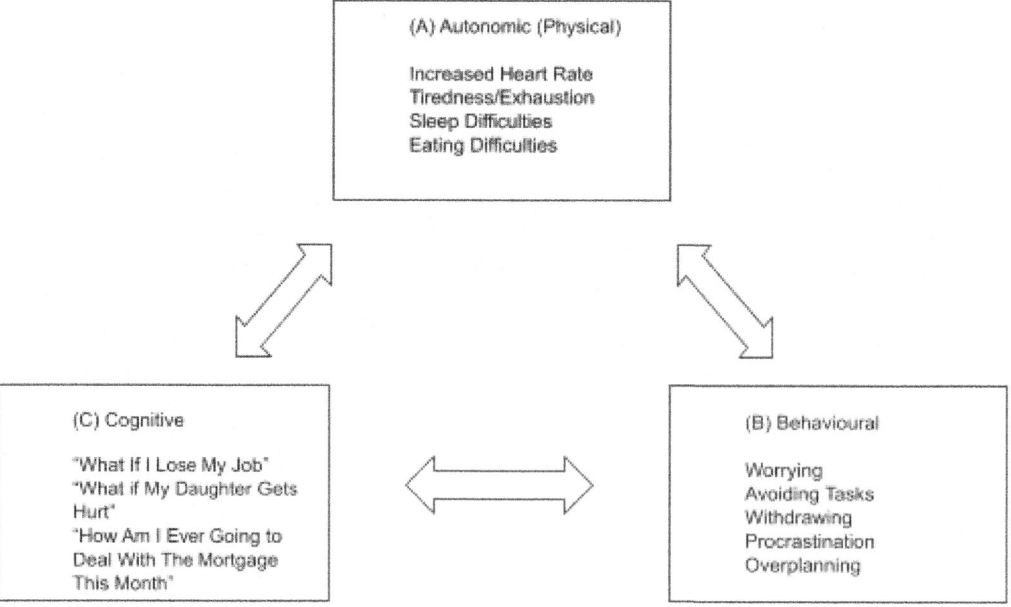

Figure 7: Example ABC cycle for GAD

The ABC cycle for GAD often involves the patient experiencing a lot of "what if" worries as well as all the usual autonomic symptoms. In terms of behaviours, they can display a wide range of worry behaviours. The guide will detail these later. But the common one to focus on at step 2 is the act of worrying.

Maintenance cycle:

The maintenance cycle is an optional psychoeducation point. Many PWP's do not include this, or even know it themselves. But personally, I have found it very useful to get a patient to understand this as it allows them to apply their learning to other worry behaviours other than the act of worrying for which worry management focuses on. Any extra awareness for the patient on their main problem is always a good thing.

I have included a diagram below of this cycle. This model was created by myself due to a lack of forumulation directed for step 2 work. *Trainee Important Tip:* **_Therefore, it is not an official GAD model that is taught on the course. During OCSE's or assessments only use the points your university instructs you too._**

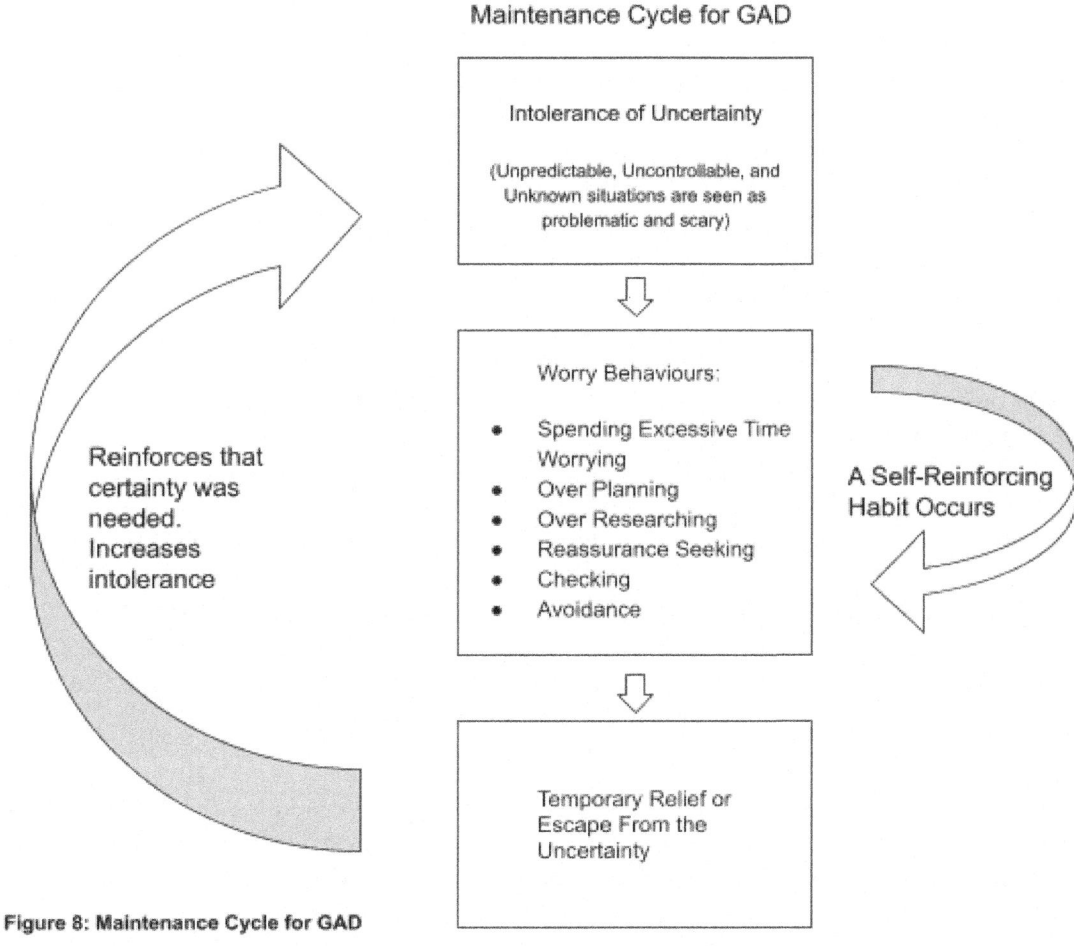

Figure 8: Maintenance Cycle for GAD

Intolerance of uncertainty is where an individual finds uncertain situations scary, hard or intolerable. Everyone has a different tolerance to uncertainty, which changes based on the situation. For example, think of someone who is able to tolerate this highly. They may be able to, on a whim, travel to another country on very little notice and just go exploring. While on the other side a person who does not tolerate uncertainty must plan for months every small detail of a trip. People can tolerate this differently for different areas of their life; thereby tolerating certain situations well and others poorly.

Worry Behaviours: When facing uncertainty a patient will feel distressed and feel the need to engage in worry behaviours. These behaviours all attempt to **reduce this uncertainty** but backfire and **maintain anxiety in the long term**. These can include:

- ***Spending excessive time worrying:*** This aims to **reduce the uncertainty in one's mind** by thinking of all the things that could happen to assess likelihood of what will happen (almost always backfires as this creates more uncertainty for each possible outcome thought through). People with GAD will often overestimate the likelihood of worries coming true.
- *Avoiding Situations:* This aims to reduce the uncertainty by simply not letting the bad outcome happen. Eg. you can not get into a car crash if you never get into a car.
- *Over planning:* This aims to reduce the uncertainty by reducing the amount of things that can go wrong. You often hear this from patients who often take pride in their ability to do this. Most are shocked to realise this is actually maintaining their anxiety.
- *Over researching:* This aims to reduce the uncertainty by providing more information and reducing the unknown or uncertain elements (Can backfire if the topic in question has no definitive answer).
- *Reassurance Seeking:* This aims to reduce uncertainty by providing certainty from others. This is often short lived and the anxiety quickly returns.
- *Procrastination:* This aims to reduce the uncertainty by putting it off this later. In that moment of time the issue "feels" resolved as it's a problem for later. This backfires as the issue usually grows larger and deadlines quickly arrive.
- *Checking:* Patients can often check if things are okay. This makes the patient temporarily feel better but often causes them to doubt the thing they check more. They can even start to doubt their own memory. This overlaps highly with OCD so ensure you take these cases to supervision if in doubt. An example of this: Imagine a patient who worries if their partner is cheating on them. They can check their phone for evidence. If they find nothing, does that reduce their anxiety? It might for a moment. But what about the next day, week or next time they have this same worry?
- *Not delegating tasks:* It can be hard to delegate if you are unsure if someone will do the task right or not.
- *Distraction:* Always having to keep "busy" to stop thinking about the worries.

There are many other worry behaviours that exist. Typically the one we focus on at step 2 is the act of worrying. If other worry behaviours are present, a step up may be required.

🍎 *Trainee Tip: I do not recommend going through all the worry behaviours with a patient. These are more for the therapist's awareness. If a patient was to mention they do any of these then you can link it to the cycle for educational purposes as mentioned above. Good psychoeducation of the intolerance of uncertainty maintenance cycle is sometimes all that is needed for patients to attempt to reduce them on their own during step 2 treatment. This is up to your discretion and only do what you feel competent for. As a trainee I would not recommend trying to work on worry behaviours which the training doesn't cover. For typical step two working only the act of worrying is focused on.*

Temporarily Relief:

When a patient engages in these behaviours they get a sense of relief. This can be as small as a feeling they have done something to help, to full blown relief (usually when avoiding).

However, as you can see from all of these examples, reducing uncertainty by using these worry behaviours never works long term. It makes the patient **less able to tolerate the uncertainty next time**. So they try to control it again, using more worrying behaviours. Using this model, anxiety is self reinforcing and without treatment can maintain itself for a lifetime (You have probably heard someone say at some point "I have been a worrier my whole life"). The patient needs to learn to tolerate the uncertainty by not engaging in worry behaviours.

Step 2: Worry Distinction: Hypothetical and Practical:

There are two main categories of worries. Both of these worries are treated differently.
Hypothetical: Worries for which there is **no realistic solution**. The worry is outside of the patient's control.

Practical: Worries for which a **realistic solution is possible**. The worry is inside of the patient's control.

Example Hypothetical Worries:

- "What if something happens to my partner?"
- "Will I lose my job?"
- "What if I get Covid?"
- "What if I mess up at work?"
- "What if I miss the deadline?"
- "What if I don't get a parking spot?"
- "What if there is traffic and I am late?"
- "What if my son/daughter/loved one gets hurt?"
- "What if my partner leaves me?"
- "What if I make my children anxious?"
- "What if my health declines?"

Example Practicals Worries:

- "How am I going to afford this bill"
- "My car just failed the MOT. How am I going to get to work tomorrow?"
- "I only have £50 left in my bank and it's the beginning of the month"
- "I have a deadline for this form I need to do".
- "I need to cancel my phone contract but I have been putting it off"

Mixed worries:
Occasionally patients will have a worry which falls a bit into both categories. In these cases it can be useful to **break down the worry** into its key parts to find out which parts are hypothetical and which parts are practical.

Are the solutions realistic:

Some patients with GAD can attempt to make any worry into a practical one. Often GAD tricks patients into thinking all of their problems have a practical solution when in reality most end up being hypothetical. Let's look at an example to illustrate the point.

Trigger: Patient has to take a plane next week.

Worry: *"What if the plane crashes?"*

For most people they realise that is hypothetical as they have no control over that situation. But if you really did some unhelpful mental gymnastics you can find some unrealistic solutions and attempt to make it practical.

1) learn to fly the plane yourself in case the pilot passes out.

2) take a parachute.

3) speak to the mechanic somehow beforehand to make sure it is all okay.

As you can see all of these are **unrealistic**. Some examples of this may not be as obviously unrealistic as this EXAMPLE. But getting the patient to look at their solutions in terms of **realism** can be helpful in getting them to realise they are hypothetical.

Also a discussion about whether or not the solution is trying to be unnecessarily preemptive before an actual problem can be helpful. This can be useful for patients who overplan as a worry behaviour.

Step 3: Worry Awareness Training (Worry Diary):

Patients with GAD can start to worry almost **automatically** without much conscious effort. They can become so efficient that they may not even be able to recognise the small things they are worried about. It's not uncommon for a patient to come into IAPT for anxiety but be unable to say what they are worried about ("I just feel anxious"). Patients can know the big things causing them to worry but have little understanding of their whole worry experience.

Worry Awareness Training is designed to give the patient a better understanding of what their triggers are, what their worries are and gives them the opportunity to classify them as hypothetical or practical.

The way we do worry awareness training at step 2 is via the use of a worry diary: see an example below.

Date and Time	Situation (Trigger)	My Worry	Anxiety level (0-10)	Hypothetical (H) or Practical (P)
28.09.2021	Writing this book	What if no one finds it interesting.	3	H
29.09.2021	About to go into my first PWP interview.	What If I mess up? Maybe I should have read that guide on how to be a PWP I saw on amazon.	7	H
28.09.2021	Need to get my car service done.	What if it has a problem?	4	H

04.10.2021	The service says my brakes need fixing	I don't have enough money for this right now. How will I be able to pay for this?	7	P
10.10.2021	I need to ask my mum for money to fix my car	This is so embarrassing. I already owe her from last time. What if she says no.	7	H
13.10.2021	My car is being fixed for a few days and I need to find a way to get to work	How am I going to get to work on time? My boss has already caught me being late a few times. What if I am late and he fires me.	6	H + P

The date and situation columns: is designed to get the patient to realise a link between events and their worries. This can sometimes help them remove or fix certain triggers. Eg. If a patient was always worrying when they first woke up and spent 15 minutes worrying in bed before they got up. A simple fix would be to get them to get up straight away and get on with their day.

The "worry" column: This section needs to be as detailed as possible and should almost mimic what goes through the patient's mind in the moment. Just simply writing *"I was worried about work"* provides little therapeutic benefit compared to *"My boss has already been caught being late a few times. What if I miss my next deadline and get fired".*

Anxiety Level: This can be a useful tool. Often a worry can span multiple weeks and seeing the anxiety level reducing can provide comfort to the patient that the treatment is beneficial even if the same worries keep reappearing. It can also help a patient realise if they have a lot of small worries which combined are leading to them feeling overwhelmed.

The last worry in the diary is an example of when a worry can seem like both a hypothetical and practical. Think through this worry based on what you have learnt in this chapter. How would you break down this worry with a patient?

Hypothetical part: What if i get fired is definitely a hypothetical worry as you can not control what your boss decides to do.
Practical part: The patient does need to find a way to work. Or a way to talk to his boss about his lateness.

Step 4: Worry Time:

Worry Time is one of my favourite skills to teach a patient. It is highly effective and works very quickly to reduce a patient's worries. It is not uncommon for patients to be lifelong worriers, then two weeks or so after using this skill to reflect that they don't feel anxious anymore.

I have heard many PWP's who do not like worrytime. I feel this comes down to them not understanding the rational or the science behind how it works. Hence why I created the formulation in this chapter.

What is Worry Time?

Worry time, also known as worry postponement, or stimulus control, is a strategy designed to allow the patient to delay and **control when and where they worry**. The patient will select a 0-20 minute window a day when they are allowed to worry but they will attempt to **contain or refocus away** from worries for the rest of the day.

The aim of this being to give the patient control back in their life, and improve quality of life and functioning. It is not designed to completely eliminate worry (an impossible feat) but in my experience, it goes a long way towards this.

Why Does it Work?

Worrytime does not have as much research base as other CBT techniques and the theoretical underpinnings are not as well understood. For more information look into "Stimulus Control" based on the Borkovec model of GAD.

However, my rationale is drawn from my knowledge and experience working with anxiety cases. For why worry time works goes back to the maintenance forumation in the start of this chapter. *Trainee Important Tip: Remember to only use the rationale provided by your university course.*

"Intolerance of Uncertainty -> Worry Behaviours -> Temporary Relief -> Increased Intolerance of Uncertainty."

This cycle has two points you can break.
1) The worry behaviours (remove that and the cycle stops):

Worry time aims to replace a patient's worry behaviour of worrying, with worry postponement. This causes the patient to realise they didn't need to worry for a few hours until worry time. They effectively stop the constant use of worry behaviours during this time which breaks the cycle.

2) The intolerance of uncertainty:

Worrytime also weakens the intolerance of certainty. When you postpone worry, you learn to tolerate it better till your worrytime. Once the intolerance of uncertainty is reduced, a patient is less likely to naturally want to engage in their worry behaviours next time, therefore weakening their intolerance of uncertainty further. It is not uncommon to find patients reacting better to uncertainty after worry time without the need to target it directly (which step 3 methods aim to do). This does not necessarily happen consciously (most PWPs never even inform a patient of intolerance of uncertainty), patients sometimes just say they simply were not feeling as worried.

Trainee Tip: Worry Time Metaphor: Cleaning the Dishes

Depending on the psychological literacy of the patient you may not be able to convey all of this knowledge about why worry time works. It is not actually needed. Many PWP just teach the steps and the patients follow on blind faith. However, having a good metaphor can go a long way in explaining this without needing to explain the whole maintenance cycle for patients to find that the strategy seems strange or has reservations about trying it.

My partner invented this metaphor which nicely demonstrates worrytime:
Imagine a parent was washing the dishes one day. Their child (aged 4-10) came up to them and asked them to play with him. What would the child do if the parent just ignored them? It would probably ask again and again, maybe it would scream and shout as they feel they are not being heard. Well that's what a worry does. If you just try to ignore it, it gets louder.

Now imagine the same situation, but instead of ignoring the child, the parent nicely and firmly told the child they would play with them in just a few minutes after they had done the dishes.The child is much more likely to go away for a few minutes till the parent came to play. This is how worry time works.

However it relies on you actually doing the worry time. If you ignored your worry and then failed to do worrytime. It's just like a parent who lied to their child. Would they listen to their parents next time they promised to play with them later?

Worrytime Steps:

Step 1: Schedule when you will have worrytime:
- Aim for 20 minutes as a good starting point. Some people may require longer. If so, aim to reduce this as time goes on.
- Aim for the evening: Around 7pm. Not too late as thinking about worries late at night could interfere with sleep.
- I wouldn't recommend the morning to start with as they leave the whole day for worries to come up and then people have to wait till the next day.
- Patients can set reminders on a phone to remind them. Consistency is key for a new habit.

Step 2: Write down worries throughout the day:
- Continue to use the worry awareness/worry diary.
- Recognise and classify them as hypothetical and practical.
- Get patients to add to their worry diary as soon as they can.

Step 3: Refocus during the day:
- Worry Time only works if you do actually contain the worries during the day.
- Do not engage in the worry or any worry behaviours.
- After you write down your worry then reflect and get back on with the day.

Step 4: Worrytime:
- ***Only for hypothetical worries.***
- Ensure the patient does distract themselves during. It needs their full focus. Do not multitask.
- Set a timer when you start so you know when to stop.
- Get rid of old worry diaries after you finish. If not then the patient will have an ever growing list of worries. New day, new diary.

- There is nothing in particular you need to do during this worry period. Just feel free to worry during this time about anything in your diary.
- If your diary has no worries, then no worrytime. Get the patient to reflect on that.

Step 5: Refocus After:
- After worrytime, the patient needs to refocus away from the worries and get back on with the day
- If a worry occurs after your worry time then they can write it in their worry diary for tomorrow.
- Start a new worry diary for the next day.

Step 5: Refocusing:

Refocusing is an important element of worry management. Worry time only works if the patient does not continue to focus or act on the worries outside of worry time.
Does that mean the patient should try to push the worry out of their mind at all costs? The answer is actually a **no**.

Trainee Tip: Pink Elephant Experiment: Many of you may have already heard of the pink elephant experiment. I often do a quick version of this with patients when discussing refocusing.

Ask the patient how many times in the last year they have thought about a pink elephant. The answer is usually zero times (Strangely, I have had two patients who have said they had).
Then ask them to try out an experiment for 15-30 seconds.
Ask them to:
   1) *Count how many times they think about a pink elephant.*
   2) *Try not to think about a pink elephant.*

Outcome:
Most patients end up thinking at least a few times about a pink elephant. This is because when we try to push something out of our mind it doesn't work. If the patient did manage to not think about a pink elephant they might be good at refocusing already and worth exploring what they were thinking/doing during the experiment.

How to refocus?:
Anxiety aims to take our focus away from the here and now and onto our worries. Refocusing using our senses or reengaging back on our day can bring us back to the moment.

Refocusing with Tasks: Patients can refocus using tasks or activities. Distraction tends to be bad if used as avoidance. However, refocusing back on the tasks at hand which you were doing before the worry occurred can be useful. Eg. If you worried at work, try to get back on with your work. It is a powerful combination with worry time because you are not ignoring the worry, you are delaying it till later.

Sight: The patient can focus on what they can see. They can make this into a small game. Get them to look for all the white objects in the room beginning with the letter "B" for example.

Touch: The patient can focus on what they can feel. If they are sitting on a hard or comfy chair; Can they feel their clothes on their skin or the floor they are standing on?

Hearing: What can they hear? Get them to focus on sounds inside or outside of their house.

Smell: This one relates to aroma, which has been shown to be highly linked to memory centres. These can help you get your mind away from the worry and in some cases help you think about something else. Consider scented candles or get them to focus on smells in the environment they are in.

Taste: Taste can be a good refocusing activity. Get the patient to try mindful eating: highly focusing on eating something while really searching for all the flavours and textures. Although be aware to not encourage the use of eating in reaction to anxiety as this can become a negative link.

Step 6: Problem Solving:

When a patient has a lot of **practical worries** the intervention used is called problem solving. This can be taught before or after worry time based on patient choice.

It is recommended to include psychoeducation about the role of avoidance and how avoiding our worries doesn't fix the issue and just delays it till later. Although patients probably intrinsically know this.

Problem solving is a highly structured set of questions aimed to get the patient to fix a practical worry.

Steps in problem solving:

1) What is my practical worry?

2) Convert this into a problem I can solve.

3) What are all the solutions?

4) What are the strengths and weaknesses of each solution?

5) Select the best solution.

6) Plan how to implement the solution.

7) Just do it!

8) Review it? What went well? What didn't?

This process can seem simple or obvious but can be a great help in dealing with problems. Let's go through each section on how the patient can complete this why it is important:

1) What is my practical worry?

The patient's worry diary should be used for this step. Only use Practical worries.

2) Convert this into a problem I can solve.

This is an important step as the patient needs to see their problem in a way that can be solved. If this step is done incorrectly it can be difficult to do the other steps. If a patient is struggling to find solutions later on, it can be good to check if they have done this step correctly.

For example: *"I have no money this month to pay my bills"* can be converted into *"I need to find an extra £100 before the end of the month"*. SMART goals can also be used here.

Trainee Tip: in my experience some patients can struggle with this. If that is the case pay extra attention to this and help the patient with a few examples.

3) What are all the solutions?

Here the patient can think of all of the possible solutions to their problem. At this point nothing is off limits. Encourage the patient to put down silly, bad or even non-legal solutions. The idea is not to do those bad ideas but they can help you think of more ideas and improve creative solutions. It is also recommended that patients put down "do nothing" or "put it off too later" as a solution. These help the patient avoid these often unhelpful solutions in the next step.

*Trainee Tip: Problem Solving is **not** about fixing the patients problems for them. The idea is to provide the framework for them to do it themselves. If the patient can not problem solve during a session, how are they going to achieve this out of the session. You can prompt solutions but always get the patient to think of ideas first.*

4) What are the strengths and weaknesses of each solution?

Now the patient can think about all the strengths and weaknesses of each solution. This should eliminate the silly, bad and non legal ones (Hopefully!... But I do live in fear that one day I will find out that an old patient of mine has robbed a bank after doing problem solving).

Usually "do nothing" or "put it off too later" seems like a bad idea at this stage as well.

Get patients to think through each solution in detail. Often patients give only surface level answers to this. But the idea is to improve their ability to produce good solutions and filter out bad ones. So the more they think about each solution the better they will be at doing this quicker in the future.

5) Select the best solution.

This step is rather easy. What does the patient feel is the best option? This can even be a mixture of solutions.

6) Plan how to implement the solution.

There is often a gap between planning and action. So the patient needs to consider actually how they are going to implement the solution. They can consider the 4 W's (What, When, Where and Who).

7) Just do it.

The next step is for the patient to go away and do the activities they have planned.

Reinforce the idea of "**Follow the plan not the feeling**". Following through is entirely up to your patient to complete.

8) Review it? What went well? What didn't?

After attempting the solution get the patient to review how it went
If it solved the problem: Great!
- Get the patient to reflect on why and learn for the future.
- Ask them if this has changed how they will deal with problems going forward.

If it did not solve the problem: Not so Great!
- Ask the patient what went wrong?
- Was it a bad solution?
- Did a barrier get in the way?
- What can they do differently next time?
- Go back and think of another solution.
- Retry the plan and overcome the barriers.

Example of all the steps in problem solving:

1) *What is my practical worry?*

I am struggling to pay my mortgage this month.

2) *Convert this into a problem I can solve?*

I need to find an extra £100 before the end of the month

3) *What are all the solutions?*

- Do nothing.
- Ignore it and hope it resolves itself.
- Rob a bank.
- Ask a friend for the money.
- Ask my family for the money.
- Pick up some extra shifts.
- Ring the bank and explain.

4) *What are the strengths and weaknesses of each solution?*

1. Do nothing:
- Strengths: None.
- Weaknesses: I will fail to make the payment.

2. Ignore it and hope it resolves itself:
- Strengths: None.
- Weaknesses: Unlikely to resolve itself on its own.

3. Rob a bank:
- Strengths: Big pay out and will never have issues paying the mortgage again.
- Weaknesses: Illegal. Wrong. I will most likely fail. My therapist will get in trouble for giving me this idea (but at least I will have a good cellmate in prison).

4. Ask a friend for the money:
- Strengths: My best friend may give it to me. Good last resort.
- Weaknesses: Would be embarrassing.

5. Ask my family for the money:
- Strengths: They would always be willing to help me.

- Weaknesses: My family have been struggling recently and it might put them under pressure.

6. Pick up some extra shifts:
- Strengths: Extra money.
- Weaknesses: Tiring and I work a lot already.

7. Ring the bank and explain:
- Strengths: It's not the first time they have probably had this issue and they might help extend it.
- Weaknesses: Seems scary and hard. Will be on hold forever.

5) *Select the best solution:*

- I think I will pick up some extra shifts at work.

6) *Plan how to implement the solution:*

- Tomorrow I will ring my boss and explain the situation and see if he has any shifts that need covering.

7) *Just do it:*

I rang my boss as planned.

8) *Review it? What went well? What didn't?*

- I rang my boss and he doesn't have any shifts for this month but has a few next month. I took him up on the offer.
- I then decided to ring the bank and explain my situation. They kindly extended the deadline to next month which I should be able to afford due to the extra shifts.

Troubleshooting for GAD:

A patient is struggling to know what type of worry they have?
- Reinforce the difference based on whether or not they can find a realistic solution to their problem.

"I can't identify my worries"

- Reinforce the use of the worry diary. Washing Machine metaphor: Sometimes our worries are like clothes spinning in a washing machine. We can see that they are there but they are spinning so fast that they just look like a blur. Doing the worry diary is like picking out one piece of clothing at a time. It takes time but in the end you will be able to see each one.
- Use physical symptoms of anxiety as a reminder/indicator to fill out your diary. Write down the situation then try to think about how you are viewing the current situation. What does the patient think is about to go wrong? That usually uncovers the worries.
- Instead of using the diary when you notice a worry throughout the day. You can use a time sampling method. Every hour or so. Write down the situation and think on any worries you have had.

Patient can not refocus:
- Go back to the rationale for why we need to refocus and come back to our worries.
- Look for refocusing activities that the patient can do.
- Get the patient to look at the benefits of trying.
- It takes practice. Get the patient to keep trying.

Patient is struggling with worrytime?
- Really reinforce the rationale for why worry time works. Often it comes down to the understanding of why they are doing it to motivate the patient.
- Explore the barriers. What is stopping the patient from doing it? Do they not understand or believe that worry time works.
- Does the case require a step up? Does the patient have some positive beliefs around worrying stopping them from wanting to postpone worrying?

Patient struggling to problem solve?
- Look at what the barrier is. If it is out of avoidance or procrastination then discuss if this will ever solve the problem?
- Spend a session focusing on 1 problem together. You can do some detailed planning with the patient on how they are going to put their selected solution into practice.
- Reframe the problem in step 2 of problem solving. Maybe the problem is too broad. SMART goals.
- It's not always about fixing the problem in its entirety. If it's a large problem. Break it down into sections which are easier to solve.
- Check it is actually a practical problem.
- Sometimes there can be no good solutions to a problem, especially if certain aspects are out of the patient's control. Only focus on what you can fix. If you can't fix the problem, maybe try to solve how you are reacting to it and how you can emotionally cope with the problem.

Problem Solving: "I know what I need to do, I just keep putting it off":

- Review if this will ever solve the problem.
- Get the patient to think of their motivation for doing it.
- Plan in a specific plan.

Trainee Tip: Remember Problem Solving is not about fixing the patients problems for them. If the patient can not problem solve during a session, how are they going to achieve this out of the session. You can prompt solutions but always get the patient to think of ideas first.

Exposure and Habituation:

Exposure and Habituation is the treatment used for Specific Phobias and Agoraphobia.

For both of these conditions the patient is actively avoiding certain situations that trigger their anxiety. This act of avoidance maintains the fear of the object or situation. Exposure aims to gradually encourage the patient to increase contact with their feared situation, in order to reduce the anxiety in the long term.

The treatment for exposure can be broken down into:
Step 1: Psychoeducation.
Step 2: Creating a hierarchy of feared situations.
Step 3: Planning exposure tasks.
Step 4: Doing the exposure tasks.
Step 5: Review and create the next task.

Step 1: Psychoeducation:

The idea of exposure can sound scary to patients. Try to imagine something you are scared of, now imagine if a therapist was about to ask you to go and face it multiple times. This is why effective psychoeducation and the rationale for exposure needs to be given.

Key Psychoeducation Points:

1) *ABC cycle:*
As with all treatments, you can link the patient's experiences to an ABC cycle to improve their awareness of their symptoms. Example ABC cycle for a dogs phobia:

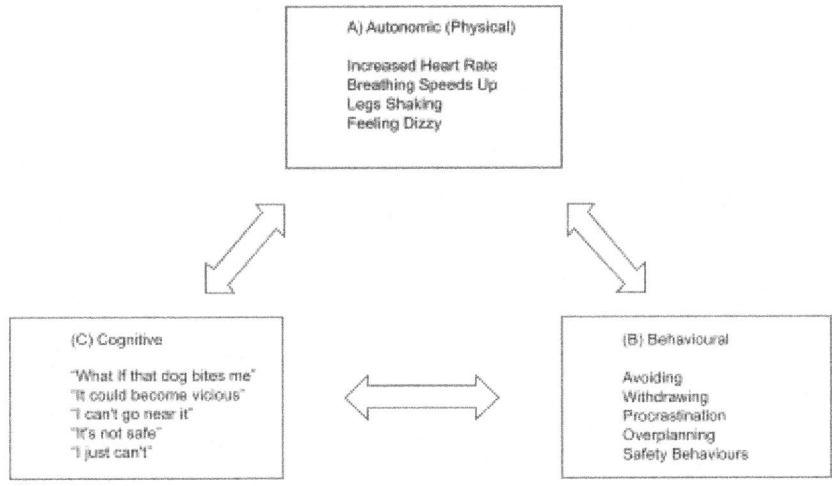

Figure 8: Example ABC cycle for a Specific Phobia

2) *The role of avoidance/escaping in maintaining the problem:*
Fear and anxiety is maintained by the act of avoiding the feared situation.

Most self help materials should have a graph similar figure 9. When faced with what is making the patient anxious, their anxiety will increase very quickly. Most patients will **avoid or escape (or use safety behaviours)** the situation. This rapidly reduces the anxiety level.

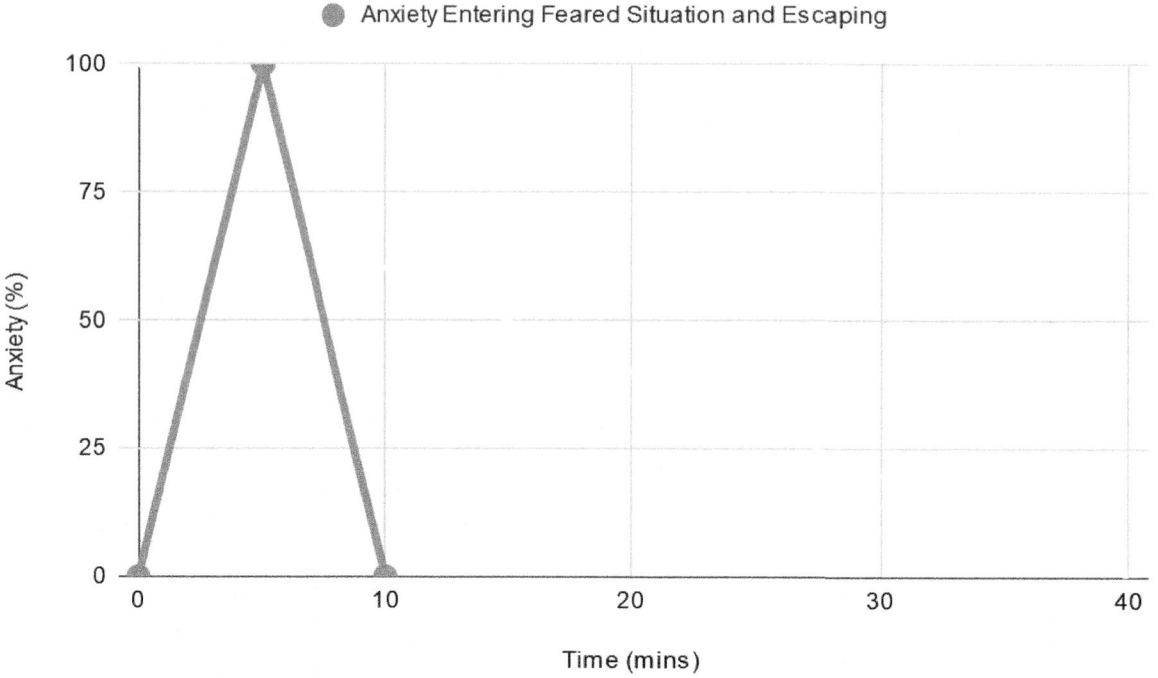

Figure 9: This graph Indicates that Anxiety quickly spikes but reduces rapidly when escaping a situation

This **maintains** the anxiety by teaching your body and brain that the feared object/situation was in fact dangerous and escape was needed (as this is what reduced the anxiety).

3) *Long term effect of this avoidance/escape*:
Therefore, next time the patient goes into that same situation **the exact pattern repeats**. The body and brain will be encouraging the patient to leave because it believes there is a life threatening danger present. The brain instead needs to learn that there is no threatening danger present and that, infact, the anxiety will come down even if we stay in the situation.
However, patients are often unaware of this. Ask the patient what they think would happen to their anxiety if they stayed in that situation?
They may say something along the lines of:
- The anxiety would go on forever.
- I wouldn't cope.
- I wouldn't be able to handle doing that.
- I will have a panic attack the whole time.

These thoughts are not accurate, which leads on to the next psychoeducation point.

4) *Anxiety does not last forever.*
Inform them about the role of **adrenaline** in anxiety and the **fight or flight response**.

Adrenaline (or Epinephrine for our American cousins) is a hormone that is designed to get our body ready for a life threatening danger. This **sparks your anxiety instantly** and is designed as a life saving mechanism to **drive you to action**. The flight or fight response doesn't like taking chances. Hence why patients feel the **intense need to escape**. Their body is reacting as if there was a real threat **when there is none**. An important thing to get patients to understand is that adrenaline only lasts temporarily. It is released in a small shot and once this runs out (after about 15-20 minutes) the intense anxiety response can no longer last as it is fuelled by adrenalin. Therefore, if you stay in a scary situation, your adrenaline will run out and your anxiety will start to reduce: your breathing will return to normal, your heart rate will return to normal etc.

The advantage of staying in the situation is that it teaches your brain that the Fight or flight response was not needed. **Nothing life threatening happened**. Therefore, in the next situation, it is **less likely to over react** or **perceive a serious threat**.

Fight or flight *(or freeze):*
The fight or flight response is an **automatic physiological reaction to an event** that is **perceived** as stressful, frightening or **life threatening**. The **perception** of threat activates the sympathetic nervous system and triggers an acute **stress response** and release of **adrenaline** that prepares the body to fight or flee this life threatening danger. See chapter on panic disorders for a detailed explanation of this. The important thing here is to discuss with the patient that this can be activated to the **perceived or imagined** threat, not only real threats.

5) *Anxiety reduction over time:*
Now the patient should have the idea that anxiety reduces over time. To help illustrate this point most self help guides will have a graph similar to the one below. This graph shows how staying in a situation works in practice.

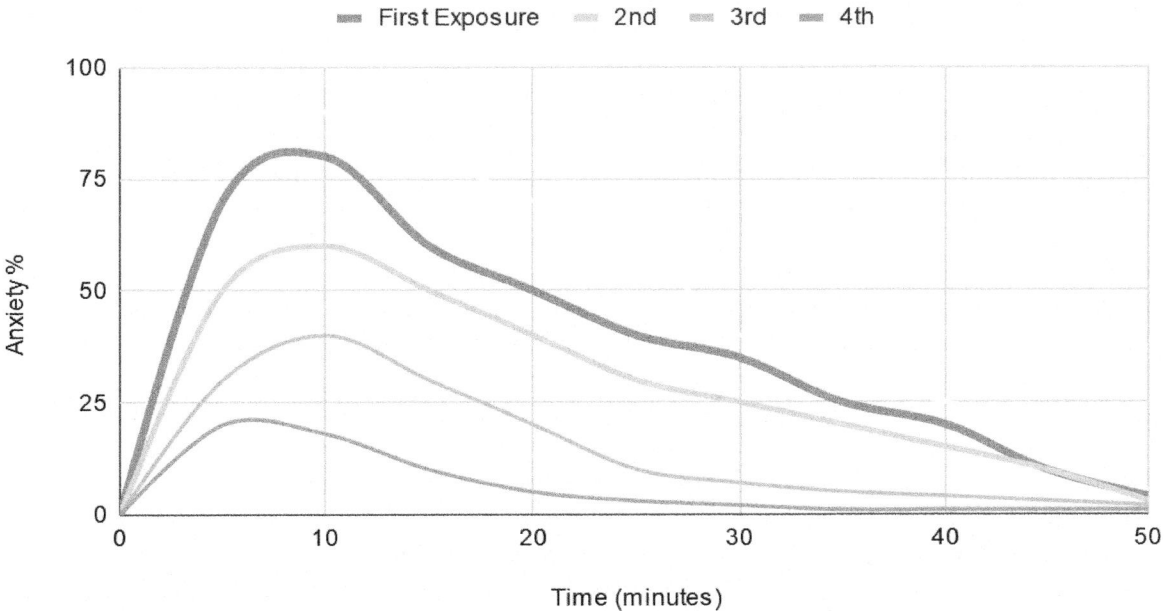

Figure 10: This Graph Indicates That Anxiety Quickly Spikes But Reduces Slowly When Staying In The Situation. Each Repeated Attempt Cause The Peak Anxiety To Reduce.

The first exposure spikes the anxiety as usual (the highest line in red) but as the person remains in the situation, it starts to taper off over the hour. Each following exposure creates less anxiety until little or no anxiety is produced when in the feared situation. This reduction in anxiety over time is called **habituation**. Habituation is when the brain gets used to a situation and no longer perceives it as dangerous. When the anxiety is no longer triggered when in the feared situation, then the patient has been fully **habituated** to the object/situation. An example of this in action is imagining watching a scary film on repeat. After a few viewings you will not be scared any more.

Some patients here may say that they occasionally go to the places or the things that they are afraid of, but they are still afraid. This is because just simply exposing yourself on its own does not create this habituation effect. There are **four conditions** which need to be met. And it is guaranteed the patient is missing at least one of them, if they are still afraid.
Condition 1: Graded.
Condition 2: Prolonged.
Condition 3: Repeated.
Condition 4: Without Distraction or Safety Behaviours.

As long as these conditions are met the patient will habituate as this is a **biological process** which is hardwired into the anatomy of the fight or flight response (Therefore, the same process also works for

most animals. *Trainee tip: Don't use this as an excuse to practice your exposure role plays on your dog, in an attempt to avoid doing role plays with other trainees).*

Condition 1: Graded:
The patient needs to do exposure slowly. If they expose themselves to the thing they are most scared of first, they often back out as it is too tough. This is called **flooding** and is seen as unethical. Flooding is often only tolerated with the use of **safety behaviours**, so typically **does not work** (see condition 4). Therefore, It is better to create a **hierarchy** of tasks building up to the harder ones (step 2 in the protocol).

Trainee Tip: Some patients' personalities might make them want to jump straight in and use the flooding technique. Remind them it is not recommended as they may find it too hard to do the other three conditions when using flooding. Therefore, they may force themselves into unnecessarily hard situations for no gain. Slow, steady and correct wins the exposure race.

Condition 2: Prolonged:
The patient needs to expose themselves for a prolonged time. If they avoid or leave the situation too early then they are just repeating their actions from the first graph where they were escaping (just on a slightly longer time frame).
The patient's anxiety needs to have dropped to about **half** of what it was at the peak/start of this exposure trial.
Only the patient can truly know when their anxiety has fallen by the right time.
Scared people are looking for any excuse to leave their feared situation. Reinforce how important it is to finish this step. Or they will have just exposed themselves and increased their anxiety for no gain. That extra 5 minutes they avoided can make the difference between habituation succeeding or failing.

Condition 3: Repeated:
Habituation needs to occur multiple times. Look at the second graph. Once was not enough.
The patient will need around 4-5 exposure trials for each step of there hierarchy

This needs to be within a short timeframe. Aim for 4-5 times in the space of a week. If a patient exposed themselves once a month for example, no habituation will occur.

Trainee tip: Patients need to be aware of the time commitment exposure requires and willing to dedicate their time. There is no point in them doing one or two exposure tasks that are too spaced out. It will just be a waste of time if the patient does not fully commit to the therapy and multiple exposure tasks in quick succession.

Condition 4: Without Distraction or Safety Behaviours:
Exposure needs to be done without any distractions. Imagine a patient who hated flying; the whole flight their eyes were closed and they were imagining they were on a bus. They will not habituate because in their mind they were not even in a plane.
This extends to anything that distracts you. Externally (your thoughts) or internally (any actions or external stimuli).

Safety behaviours (or safety seeking behaviours): A safety behaviour is anything that a patient does to help reduce their anxiety. This often helps in the short term but causes the anxiety to remain in the long term. If the patient ever had to do a task without their safety behaviour, their anxiety would spike higher. Safety Behaviours stop an individual from directly testing their fears. They don't get to see how the situation would have been without them. This impacts the patient's learning and hinders habituation. Safety behaviours can become a "self-fulfilling prophecy". Sometimes they can lead to the negative consequence they were meant to solve.
Patients can start to believe that the safety behaviour stopped there fear from coming true when it had no effect (eg. *"I didn't have a panic attack because I took my calm's tablet"*).

Anything can become a safety behaviour. But they usually follow a similar pattern;

Behavioural to "prevent":
- Avoidance
- Over preparing or planning every detail
- Only going when something indicates it is "safe"
- Reassurance Seeking prior to the situation
- Preparing to take a item with them (eg. Carrying around anti-anxiety medication just in case the worst was to occur)

Behavioural to "escape":
- Escaping/leaving the situation
- Possessing a safety item during the task (eg. I will be able to cope if i listen to music with my headphones during).
- Doing a safety action (eg. taking a sip of water when anxious)
- Reassurance seeking during the task.
- Taking a trusted person with them.
- Reducing their senses to the situation (e.g music)

Cognitive to "prevent":
- Over preparing in mind.
- Telling themselves over and over it's going to be okay.

Cognitive to "avoid/escape":
- Distraction in mind (eg. Over focusing on an object or idea).
- Trying to not think about the scary object.

🍎 *Trainee Tip: Explore safety behaviours with the patient during the IA stage when assessing for panic, specific phobias or agoraphobia. Also worth exploring with the patient again at this stage as psychoeducation. Patients often don't realise what they do is safety behaviour. Maybe get the patient to give a detailed account of a recent experience to help identify any.*

🍎 *Rather than asking "do you have any safety behaviours?", it can be worth asking the patient "what would you usually do to cope during these types of situations?".*

🍎 *Some safety behaviours can overlap with OCD symptoms such as neutralising in head or compulsions. Take to supervision if OCD is suspected.*

Step 2: Creating a hierarchy of feared situations.

Graded Exposure:
Once the patient understands all the psychoeducation points above they are ready to understand and start using graded exposure.
The next step in treatment is for the patient to create a hierarchy of feared situations. This is to fulfil the graded condition of exposure. The patient selects their most feared situation. Then creates less fearful tasks building up to that situation. The patient rates how much anxiety from 0-100% they believe this situation causes. Ensure the anxiety rating is at least 40% or higher. Anything less than 40% does not warrant exposure.

🍎 *Trainee Tip: Some patients have multiple feared situations or phobias. Only focus on one during a hierarchy. It would be pointless for a spider phobia hierarchy to also include tasks involving heights for example.*

🍎 *Trainee Tip: You can create exposure tasks around removing safety behaviours. Eg. one task could be to go to the shops with their friend. Then the next to go to the shops alone.*

Here is an example of a filled out exposure hierarchy: The patient will start with exposure to the easiest tasks on 4-5 occasions until the situation causes minimal anxiety. Then move up to harder tasks once they feel they are no longer that anxious in the previous situation.

Difficulty	Task	Anxiety Rating (0-100%)
Most difficult	Going on the underground during rush hour in central London	100%
Difficult	Going on the london underground in central London	90%

Medium	Going on the underground on a non busy outer line	75%
Medium	Going to the platform on the underground	60%
Easy	Going into the underground tunnels	55%
Easiest	Standing at the entrance to the underground	40%

Step 3: Planning exposure tasks:

Once the patient has done their hierarchy it is now time to plan the first exposure task.
It is best to have a detailed and concrete plan on the task they will do. As previously mentioned, exposure can be scary. A well crafted plan can provide the motivation to proceed. Aim for the patient to create their own tasks but guide them to ensure they considered the 4 conditions.

Condition 1: Graded: The patient should choose something that causes approximately at least 40-50% anxiety to start with.
Condition 2: Prolonged: Ask them if they remember how long they need to do it for. Till the anxiety is reduced by half.
Condition 3: Repeated: Ask them how many times and when they are going to do the task. Explore any barriers to achieving this (eg. time, access, motivation).
Condition 4: Without Distraction or safety behaviours. Go into detail about anything that could distract the patient.

Step 4: Doing the exposure tasks:

It is up to the patient to actually follow through with their exposure tasks.
They can record their progress in a diary.

Most exposure materials will provide a blank diary. It should contain:
Filled out before exposure:
1. Date of time
2. A section to plan the task
Filled out after each exposure task:
3. The duration the task lasted
4. Self reported anxiety 0-100% before the task started
5. Self reported anxiety 0-100% at the end of the task
6. A section for the patient to comment and reflect on any learning from the task.

Here is an example of a filled out diary.

Date and Time	Planned Task	Duration Lasted (minutes)	Anxiety at start of Task %	Anxiety at end of the task %	Comments

Monday	Going into the underground tunnels.	90m	55%	25%	That was so scary but I managed it. Noticed i tried to distract myself by over focusing on the posters on the walls.
Tuesday	Going into the underground tunnels.	80m	45%	20%	Still didn't like it but it seemed easier this time. Didn't distract self at all
Thursday	Going into the underground tunnels.	45m	25%*	15%	I barely worried
Saturday	Going into the underground tunnels.	10m	15%	5%	Not actually bad now.
Monday	Going to the platform on the underground	90m	60%	30%	Very scared but I know it will get better

As you can see the patient clearly stated what activity they were going to expose themselves too and it met the 4 conditions.
1. It was graded: They started off with an easy task.
2. It was prolonged: The first time was for 80m and the patient stayed there anxiety halved.
3. It was repeated: They attempted it on 4 occasions before moving on to a new one.
4. It was without distraction: The patient noticed on the 1st occasion their safety behaviour and stopped this for the following tasks.

The third trial showed that the patient's anxiety when starting was below 40%. This is a good indication that the patient has already habituated and could have moved on to the next task. Therefore the 4th attempt was most likely not required (as seen as the anxiety only starting at 15%).

Step 5: Review and plan the next task:

Once the patient has done their exposure task enough times that their anxiety has fallen by half. They can plan their next exposure task from the hierarchy.
Depending on the length of the hierarchy, it is not uncommon for a patient to have not reached the top of their hierarchy before treatment ends. Therefore, it is so important for the patient to have all the skills, knowledge and ability to continue to plan and carry out their exposure tasks without therapist input.
The patient can start to reflect on their experiences of what is working and not working when exposing themselves. This is important to update there knowledge of their feared situation eg. If they have been exposing themselves to dogs and the original fear was that all dogs are dangerous. Do they still believe this?

Troubleshooting for Exposure:

"I do face my fears already but I am still scared":
- Often patients will not completely avoid their feared situation. Due to this they can feel that exposure wouldn't work as they believe they are already exposing themselves.
- Often they are missing at least 1 of the 4 conditions required. Explain to the patient that this is why they are still afraid. Explore past examples with the patient.
- Ensure the patient is not flooding themselves.
- Screen for trauma. Other considerations are present and should be seen at step 3.

No improvement during treatment:
- Check if the patient is actually doing their homework
- Check for Safety Behaviours. Patients may not be aware of them during exposure tasks.
- Check all 4 conditions are being met.
- Check if the patient is on any Anxiety Medication. This can stop habituation and is similar to a safety behaviour.
- Is the patient not moving up their hierarchy out of fear?

Not doing homework:
- Explore the barriers as usual.
- Exposure can be scary. Assess the patient's motivation for change.
- Exposure requires the patient to do it. There is no point continuing with sessions if the patient is not ready. Check if the patient is the right time for therapy.

Not enough time for exposure:
- Exposure can be very time consuming. The patient has to go to their feared location 4-5 times in the space of a week and stay for a prolonged time.
- Assess motivation for change. It requires a time commitment.
- Discuss how important it is with the patient to overcome their fear. The patients may need to make time or go out of their way to achieve this. Eg. Take time off work etc.

Panic Disorder:

Panic treatment is aimed to get the patient to understand what causes a panic attack and to change the way they view their panic symptoms and experience.
This treatment is highly dependent on psychoeducation.

Sometimes just this education is enough to stop panic attacks. So ensure you are delivering this knowledge well.

Before starting with any panic management treatments, always check that the patient has ruled out any physical health issues causing the symptoms.

If the patient is pregnant some services will not advise exposure. Check this out with your individual service.

Treatment Steps:

Step 1: Psychoeducation: The first step in treating panic is to provide really good psychoeducation on:
- What causes a panic attack.
- ABC cycle
- Fight or flight response
- The role of adrenaline
- That panic attacks are caused by a misinterpretation of symptoms

Step 2: Panic Diary.
Step 3: Alternative Explanations (form of cognitive restructuring).
Step 4: Reducing safety behaviours and/or internal focus of attention.

Step 1: Psychoeducation:

What is a panic attack:
A panic attack is a strong rush of intense physical and cognitive symptoms of anxiety. It can come on quickly and sometimes for no apparent reason. Using an ABC cycle can help both you and the patient understand their panic experience better.

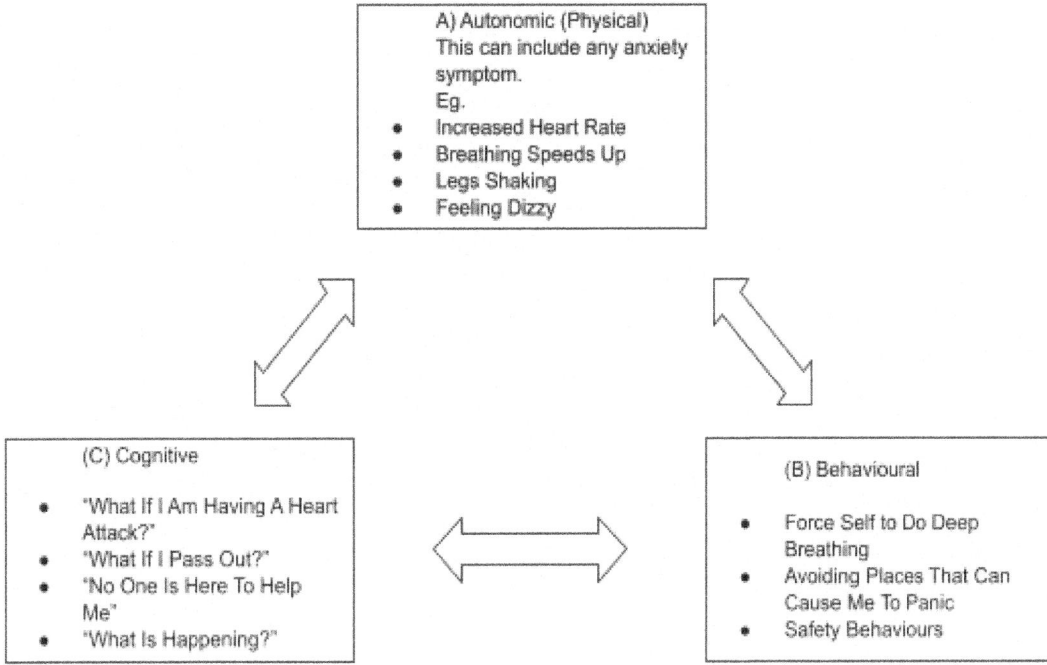

Figure 11: Example ABC cycle for Panic Disorder.

What causes a panic attack:
A panic attack is caused by catastrophic **misinterpretations** of symptoms in which a person worries overly about the meaning behind their physical symptoms. This worry intern **causes the anxiety symptoms to worsen**.

The Clark model of panic:
This model is more often used in step 3 treatments but it is a simple enough model that it can be used at step 2.

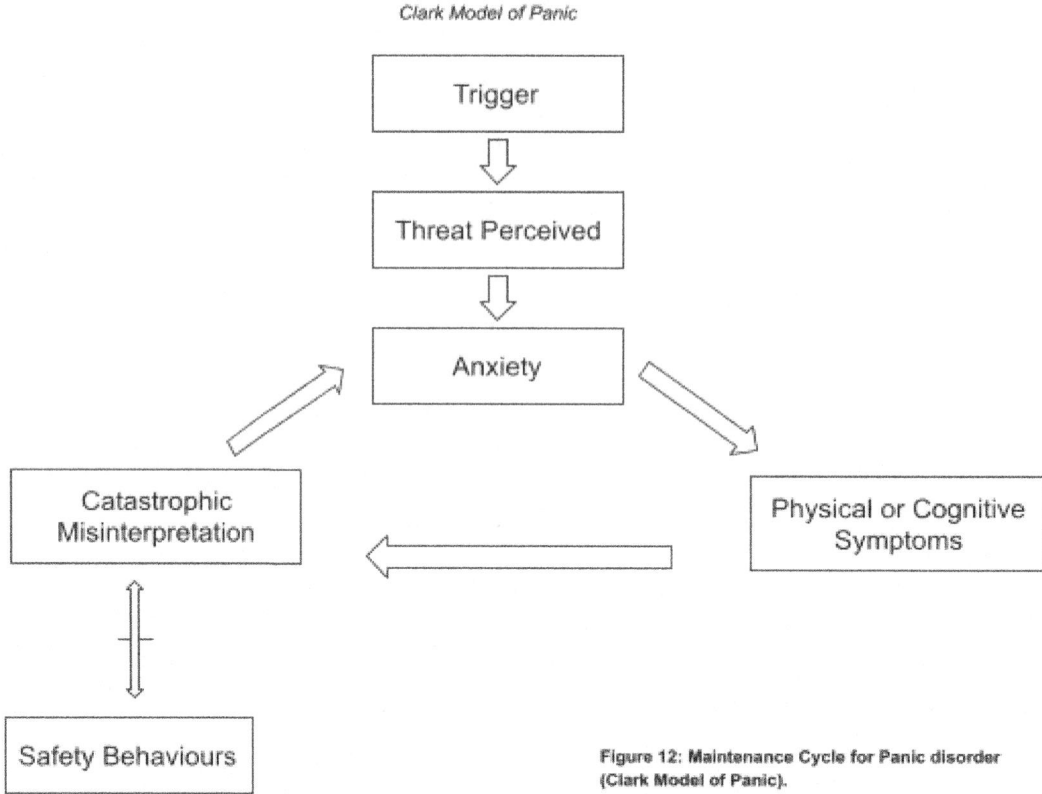

Figure 12: Maintenance Cycle for Panic disorder (Clark Model of Panic).

This diagram shows the steps in what causes a panic attack.

A **trigger** occurs. This can be internal (a physical symptom) or an external trigger of anxiety. This causes the person to **perceive** that there is a threat. This causes **anxiety** and activates the **Fight or Flight Response**. This causes a range of **physical and cognitive symptoms**. The patient then **misinterprets the meaning** of these symptoms as **dangerous, strange and alarming**. This causes more anxiety and the cycle continues.

Often before or during a panic attack, patients engage in **safety behaviours**. These can reduce anxiety in the short term but maintain anxiety in many main ways.

- The person can believe that they were only safe due to the intervention of the safety behaviour they engaged in (e.g. If i didn't lie down when I felt the panic coming on, I would have had a full blown panic attack).
- Safety Behaviours over time can reinforce the incorrect belief that their symptoms were dangerous.
- They can directly increase the symptoms of anxiety (e.g. Selective Attention where a person scans and constantly looks out for any worrisome symptoms).

Example of the Clark model in practice:

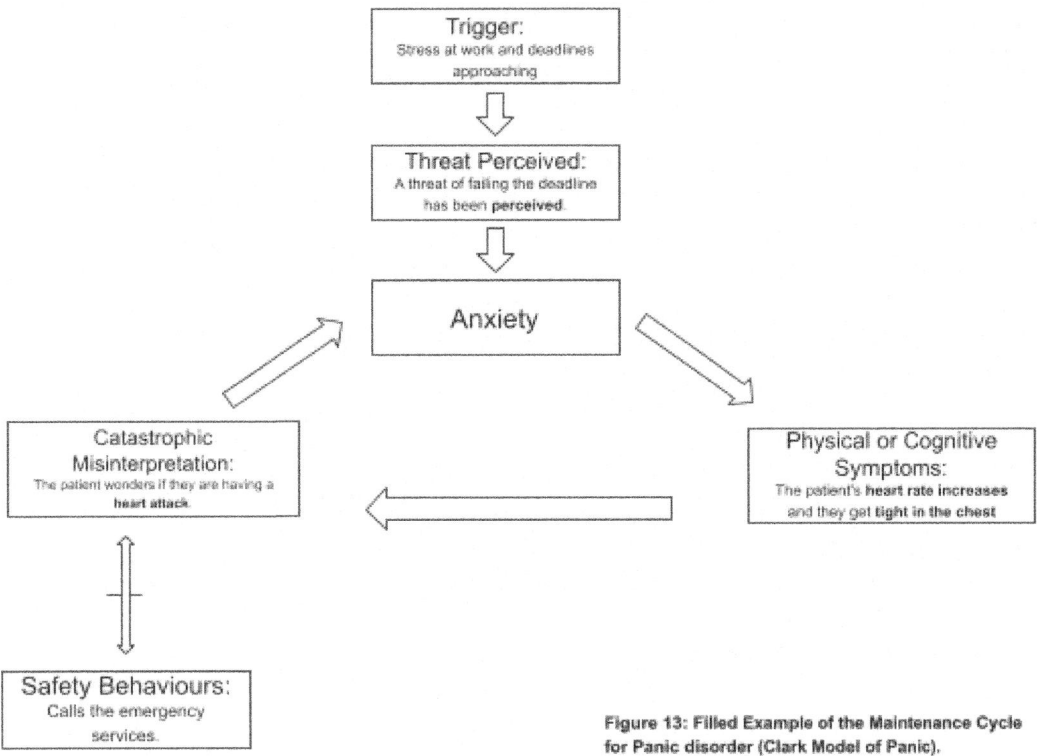

Figure 13: Filled Example of the Maintenance Cycle for Panic disorder (Clark Model of Panic).

Trigger: Stress at work and deadline approaching.
Threat Perceived: A threat of failing the deadline has been **perceived**.
Anxiety: The patient has become **anxious** about it.
Physical or Cognitive Symptoms: The patient's **heart rate increases** and they get **tight in the chest**.
Catastrophic Misinterpretation: The patient recognises the increase in heart rate and tight chest but **fails to realise that it was caused by** stress around the approaching deadline. The patient wonders if they are having a heart attack (**Catastrophic Misinterpretation**).

This leads to:
More anxiety and an **increase in heart rate and tightness in the chest occurs**.
This acts as confirmation for the patients catastrophic misinterpretation and the cycle continues and worsens.
Due to this the patient engages in safety **behaviour** and calls the emergency services.

Are panic attacks harmful?
No. It is simply the fight or flight response doing its job. And that job is to keep you alive so it wouldn't make sense for it to have the ability to cause harm.

Can you pass out?
No*. If a patient has said this has actually occurred then they need to speak to their GP about an underlying medical condition such as low blood pressure. During the fight or flight response, a person's blood pressure increases which inhibits the ability to pass out (which requires a lowering of blood pressure). The only exception* to this, is if the patient has underlying low blood pressure, a **needle or blood phobia**. It is theorised that when seeing blood, a person's brain can interpret the situation as if they themselves were having major blood loss. Therefore, it causes the body to drop down to the floor so that

the injury is on level with the heart in an attempt to reduce blood loss. It can also be a part of the freeze response.

Flight or fight (or freeze) response:
Inform the patient of the fight and flight response and the role of adrenaline.
The fight or flight response is an **automatic physiological reaction to an event** that is **perceived** as stressful or frightening. The **perception** of threat activates the sympathetic nervous system and triggers an acute stress response and release of **adrenaline** that prepares the body to fight or flee. The important thing here is to discuss that this can be activated to the **perceived** threat, not such real threats. **This includes the fight and flight response misinterpreting its own symptoms**.

Adrenaline is a hormone that is designed to get our body ready for a threat. This sparks your anxiety instantly and is designed as a life saving mechanism to drive you to action.

During panic attacks, it is adrenaline causing an increase in symptoms which the patient is misinterpreting, which causes more adrenaline to be released.
Their body is reacting as if there was a real threat **when there is none** based on a **misinterpretation**. An important thing to get the patients to understand is that adrenaline is time limited and that the **symptoms caused are not harmful**. It is designed for short bursts of activity. Adrenaline will slowly run out over the course of an hour and you will feel less anxious as the time goes on. Panic attacks end on their own once the body has exhausted itself (or the patient engages in a safety behaviour or calms down).

Step 2: Panic Diary:

The next step is for both the patient and therapy to find out more about what symptoms the patient is presenting with. For this, the patient should fill out a panic diary to record any panic attacks they are having. Most self help materials will have a chart similar to the one below.

It should include:
- The situation.
- What anxiety symptoms were present.
- How the symptoms were interpreted.
- The patient's response to the situation.

Here is a filled out example:

Date and Time	Situation	Main body sensation	How did I Interpret this symptom	How did I react? What did I do?	How long the panic lasted
03/10/2021	Woke up in middle of the night and couldn't breathe	Felt a shortness of breath	I cant breath I thought i was suffocating	Jumped out of bed and ran outside for air	3 minutes and stopped shortly after I got the

					garden
05/10/2021	Was at work in the office working on my pc for a few hours straight	Starting to get a headache. Then my vision went strange. Felt faint	Thought there was something wrong with my brain. Maybe a stroke or a tumour	Panicked and my co-workers called for an ambulance	10 minutes
07/10/2021	Woke up after a nightmare	Felt numb in my right arm and my heart was racing	I thought i was having a heart attack	My wife calmed me down and told me it was nothing. She got me to do some deep breathing	15 minutes

Step 3: Alternative Explanations (form of cognitive restructuring):

After reviewing the diary, explore what the patient interpretation of symptoms is and then provide psychoeducation about how these symptoms are produced by the fight and flight response and their **intended** functions. See list below which covers some of the most common symptoms.

Symptom Of Fight And Flight	*Common Catastrophic Misinterpretations*	*Actual Function Or Cause In The Fight Or Flight Response.*
Shortness Of Breath Or Rapid Breathing	I will stop breathing and pass out	Breathing quickens to improve oxygen supply. This can cause rapid breathing but can also lead to tightness in the chest or even a sensation of shortness of breath. This shortness of breath is just a sensation, and you are in fact getting enough oxygen
Racing Heart Palpitations	I am having a heart attack	Heart rate increase to improve blood supply
Chest Pain	I am having a heart attack	Increased muscle tension in chest due to increased breathing
Lump In Throat And/Or Difficulty Swallowing	What if I choke?	Saliva production is not a vital function and deduces, making it harder to swallow.
Skin Losing Colour	What's wrong with me? Am I going into shock? Am I not getting enough oxygen?	Blood is being diverted from skin to vital organs
Neck, Shoulder Pain Or Numbness In Face Or Head	Am I having a stroke?	Increased muscle tension due to adrenaline
Sweating	Is something wrong with me?	To cool the body down in

		preparation for action
Weakness In Arms Or Tingling In The Hands Or Feet	Am I having a stroke or heart attack?	Due to increased breathing to increase blood flow to vital organs. The oxygen to carbon dioxide levels in the blood can temporarily change. Causing these symptoms as a side effect.
Heartburn, Constipation Or Diarrhoea	I'm going to wet myself and embarrass myself in public	The body shuts down non vital organs temporarily. Who needs to digest a meal when your body is getting ready to run.
Shaking	I'm going to faint or collapse	The body is getting the muscles ready to quickly spring into action.
Dry Mouth	What if I choke?	Fluids are diverted to other parts of the body
Racing Thoughts	I'm losing my mind	Adrenaline causes your mind to speed up and can cause thoughts to race.
Fears Of Going Mad Or Losing Control	I'm going 'crazy'	Racing thoughts or feeling out of control are common when adrenaline is rushing through your system. This is an unintended side effect. You can not go mad or lose control. Going mad is not a conscious act.
Distorted Vision	I'm going blind	Your vision changes to look out for any threats. This can cause tunnel vision.
Pain In The Face Or Jaw.	Am I having a stroke?	Muscle tension in the face increases due to adrenaline
Derealisation And Depersonalisation	I'm losing my mind	Somepeople freeze during the fight or flight response. It is designed to help you stay inactive when hiding. Adrenaline and racing thoughts can add to this feeling.
Headaches	Do I have a tumour or brain haemorrhage?	Muscle tension in the face and head increases due to adrenaline

It is very important to get the patient to realise the **function behind these symptoms**. Because during a panic attack they are **misinterpreting** them. If they can realise they are not **harmful or scary** but a **normal function** of the body, they will not misinterpret and the panic will not occur.

Thought challenging: Once the patient understands the function of the symptoms and what misinterpretation they are having they can start challenging this either before, during or after a panic attack.

They can ask themselves questions such as:

1) What is my anxiety trying to tell me this symptom means? (The misinterpretation: eg. Is it a heart attack?)
2) What would this symptom mean if it was just the fight or flight response?
3) Which interpretation is more likely?
4) To try to rationale the situation. Eg. They can remind themselves that it wasn't a heart attack the last 10 times they had a panic attack. So what are the chances it is now?

A more detailed panic diary can be helpful to get the patient to think about the alternative explanation for their symptoms. See bellow:

Date and Time	Situation	Main body sensation	How did I Interpret this symptom	How could I interpret this if it was just anxiety	Did I do any safety behaviours	How long the panic lasted

Look at the same examples from the last chart in this new chart below. Imagine the patient knew more about their panic symptoms and challenged them in the moment. Their diary may look different:

Date and Time	Situation	Main body sensation	How did I Interpret this symptom	How could I interpret this if it was just anxiety	Did I do any safety behaviours	How long the panic lasted
03/10/2021	Woke up in middle of the night and couldn't breathe	Felt a shortness of breath	I cant breath I thought i was suffocating	It is just anxiety. I will not suffocate	I did some deep breathing but I realised I was going to be fine regardless	3 Minutes
05/10/2021	Was at work in the office working on my pc for a few hours straight	Starting to get a headache. Then my vision went strange. Felt	Thought there was something wrong with my brain.	I was just working too hard and got a headache. I have been	No. I simple took a break which Was much needed	1 Minute

		faint	Maybe a stroke or a tumour	staring at a PC screen for hours and my eyes were tired		

Step 4: Reducing safety behaviours or internal focus of attention:

Safety Behaviours:
The role of safety behaviours and how reducing these will actually help reduce panic attacks in future should be explored. Explore safety behaviours with patients and try to get them to realise that this may not be as helpful as they believe. Patients need to confirm that their cataphopsic misinterpretation of symptoms is wrong and that their new way of thinking that "it is just anxiety" is correct. Explain how safety behaviours stop this learning from happening.

Internal focus of attention:
Another key feature of panic is an increased internal focus of attention. **This is treading on step 3 treatments** but it can be useful to provide minor psychoeducation around this. When a patient gets panic attacks they can become **highly attune to their physical symptoms**. They can scan or look out for them. This is as they perceive them as a threat or an indication that a panic attack is about to occur. Many patients will tell you they can *"feel a panic attack before it happens"*. That is a red flag that they are internally focusing their attention. This scanning can cause panic attacks, as everyone can find (or cause) strange physical sensation if they are looking for them. An example from step 3 treatment is getting the patient to highly focus on a part of the body (usually their foot) and the patient will usually notice sensations they didn't notice before the scanning. This occurs for panic patients during their day and they misinterpret them, causing panic. For step 2 treatment, it is advised to just inform the patient of how this works and the rationale for how this can cause panic attacks. And see if the patient can naturally reduce engaging in this.

 A good analogy of this is a "Faulty car alarm" that goes off when the wind blows. The car alarm needs to be turned down. The patient's internal alarm is set so sensitive due to this internal focus of attention that every little sensation can trigger it. Getting the patient to realise this and try to stop focusing internally can help reduce panic attacks.

Other considerations:

Reduce stress in life:
It can be worth exploring ways to reduce or cope with stress in the patient's life. This can reduce the initial anxiety symptoms from triggering panic. *Remember: Get the patient to realise that even if they were stressed, they wouldn't have a panic attack if they didn't misinterpret the "dangerousness" of the symptoms.*

Distraction:

Distraction can be an effective way of dealing with panic as it can distract the patient from thinking or misinterpreting symptoms during. _It is very important to get the patient to realise that distraction is not preventing the panic or something bad from happening_. The opposite is true, it shows that nothing bad was actually going to happen. **How could a distraction stop a heart attack?** _Distraction can be a safety behaviour when used incorrectly_. Only use distraction as a way to demonstrate or prove it is anxiety once the patient understands the cycle of panic and their symptoms are not dangerous.

Relaxation and Breathing:
Relaxation and Breathing techniques can be effective for dealing with panic. It can reduce the physical sensations of panic, thereby reducing the chances of misinterpreting them. _It is very important to get the patient to realise that relaxation or breathing techniques are not preventing the panic or something bad from happening. Even if the patient did not do these breathing exercises, nothing dangerous is going to occur._

Troubleshooting for Panic:

Patient struggling to challenge their catahopsic misinterpretation:
- Review evidence for and against. Check they are using factual evidence and not feelings.
- Go into detail what the patient fears will happen, and challenge each part separately.
- The patient may need to do a behavioural experiment. This is not taught on the national curriculum and is often seen as a continual professional development after qualification. Step up to step 3 may be required.
- Has the patient seen a GP? They need to rule out a real health problem before getting them to see it as just anxiety.

No improvement during treatment:
- Check if the patient is actually doing their homework,
- Check if the patient still believes their misinterpretation.
- Check for Safety Behaviours. Patients may not be aware of them.
- Check if the patient is on any Anxiety Medication. This can be a safety behaviour.
- Check if the patient is refocusing when anxious. They may still be internally focusing.
- Is the patient avoiding anything? If so then exposure may be required.
- Has the problem transitioned to a fear of panic attacks rather than them actually occurring.
- Does the patient understand all the psychoeducation? Ask them to walk you through what they understand.

Not doing homework:
- Explore the barriers
- Is it the right time for therapy?
- Assess motivation for change. It requires a time commitment.

Patient hasn't had the opportunity to use the strategies as not had a panic attack for a while:
- Some patients when starting treatment state they haven't had a panic attack in a few weeks/months. This is a red flag that the patient may not have panic disorder. People reporting having panic attacks are common, but may not need to be treated as panic disorder.
- It could be that they have a worry problem instead. They can worry about having a panic attack. Reassess the goals and presenting symptoms with the patient.

- Another red flag is if the patient states they have panic that lasts for hours. Panic attacks are acute and not prolonged. This indicates they most likely have another anxiety disorder (or are just very stressed).

Other health considerations:
- If the patient has a heart or lung condition they need to know how to differentiate between panic and a flare up.
- This will be covered after qualification during the long term health condition training. Use supervision or clinical skills for this in the meantime.

Computerised Cognitive Behavioural Therapy (cCBT)

Computerised Cognitive Behavioural Therapy (cCBT) is not a core part of the PWP training program. However, many services use at least one form of this. Silvercloud is the most common program currently.

cCBT is often an online course designed to help patients manage common mental health disorders such as anxiety and depression, but may also focus on stress, sleep, relationships and self esteem. Patients usually work through a series of topics selected by the PWP to address their specific needs. These courses are designed to be completed in the patient's own time and at their own pace. The courses often feature videos, activities, quizzes, audio guides and an online journal.

This can also be in two forms:

- Pure self help: The patient is often discharged and goes through the course independently.
- Guided self help. A PWP will check in with the patient's progress at regular intervals to review their progress and reinforce engagement with the program.

Some people find cCBT helpful, but it's not suitable for everyone. It may feel right for some people but not others who prefer human contact during sessions. The motivation of the patient is highly important. Patients can choose cCBT just to stop using it after a week or so if not motivated.

Interview Tip: Knowing that cCBT exists and is an option can help you stand out in interviews. You don't need to know much about them in detail.

Trainee Tips:

- *Using cCBT is a good way to manage caseloads. Review sessions are typically quicker than usual treatment sessions.*
- *cCBT is often designed to be a stand alone treatment. Don't complicate it by bringing in external materials or bombarding the patient with additional advice. The aim is to direct them back to the program and enhance engagement in the cCBT.*
- *cCBT usually requires more motivation for the patient to engage. Consider barriers such as motivation for patients before starting a course of cCBT.*

Signposting:

Thinking back to the stepped care model. An important element of a PWP's role is to signpost patients who may not benefit from IAPT interventions to other relevant services. This doesn't just refer to stepping up and down within the NHS, but can be in the form of professional referrals to external services, or to informing a patient of a service for them to contact independently.

This is important for improving access to services that can complement or run parallel to IAPT treatment. This can include services such as employment support, volunteering, exercise, or directing the patient to speak to their GP.

Signposting to charity organisations is also common.

Common signposting will be to:
- Counselling: CBT will not be the preferred modality for everyone. Sometimes patients want to talk through things. Patients with trauma or previous abuse may also benefit from processing the trauma via counselling prior to CBT if the patient has never confronted what happened.
- Bereavement: Bereavement is often not suitable to be seen in IAPT. Most grief will subside naturally with time. Should this be the patient's main problem, external specialist services may be superior to guided self help.
- Cancer: Lifetime cancer rates are approaching 1 in 2. This makes knowing cancer signposting very relevant. Both for patients or for their loved ones.
- Employment Support: One of the key aims of IAPT is to get patients back into work. Many IAPT services have a dedicated team to aid with this.

Other examples can include:

- Abuse
- Alcohol and drugs
- Baby Groups for parents
- Benefits/Universal Credit
- Developmental and neurodevelopmental disorders
- Housing support
- LTC

- LGBT
- Sensory issues. Eg. hearing, sight
- Older adults
- Pregnancy support
- Couple counselling
- Veterans
- Young persons services
- Work support (bullying at work)

Digital Signposting: The COVID pandemic has drastically changed the digital landscape for mental health support. Many services and charities have started introducing webinars and online workshops. It has yet to be seen if this will persist in the long term. Knowing the availability of these webinars can be useful for patients as this allows them to engage from the comfort of their own home.

Interview tip: Being aware that signposting is a vital part of the role is advised. This will show the interviewers you have researched the job role in detail. No need to know how or any specific services.

Trainee Tips:

- *Become aware of the various signposting opportunities as soon as possible. When the job first starts the caseloads are low, so use this time to explore signposting. Ask other PWPs where they signpost. Services often have a document of signposting opportunities. If not, create your own.*
- *Sometimes patients will not be suitable for service. It can feel uncomfortable informing a patient they are not getting treatment. Having signposting ready for these times can be useful.*

Module Two Summary:

This concludes the information for chapter two.
By this point you should have as good idea regarding:
- What guided self help is.
- How a typical treatment session is structured.
- What treatment is used for each disorder.
- A rough understanding of all the steps used for each treatment.

Interview Stage: As mentioned before, you are not expected to know much about these treatments. Knowing the names is more than enough. To really shine in the interview, read through the interview section again and try to memorise the small summary.

Trainee Before Lectures in Module Two: As mentioned before, module two moves very fast. Read each section prior to your lecture on that particular treatment. The more you know in advance the better. Don't worry if you don't fully understand a treatment prior to your lecture. Going in with even a bit of knowledge prior is really helpful. I would recommend looking into what self help guides your service recommends and giving them a read.

Trainee After Lecture on Treatment: Hopefully you found the university lecture very informative. Read the section on the treatment you have just learnt again. Really try to understand the rationale and steps. Do a lot of role plays and shadow some real sessions. Good luck with your first real treatment session. Just remember the patient does not know what to expect. So just try your best and soon you will be much more comfortable and competent.

Module Three: Values, Employment and Context

IAPT aims to improve access to psychological therapies. This includes being inclusive and respecting the diversity of all patients. Diversity encompassess a range of culurtal normals, ranging from religion, cultural, personal, family and social values. Services need to also take into account any physical difficulties making access to the service difficult and attempting to mitigate these barriers. This module also explores any unconscious biases, and aids the recognition of limitations to your competences. It explores inclusion, multiculturalism and equips you with the knowledge of how to work in a culturally competent manner. This module also provides an awareness into the power dynamics between the therapist and the patient, and on how to take steps to reduce any potential negative impacts of this.

During this stage of the training you will often be increasing your caseloads from a trainee level to approximately 60-80% of a qualified PWP. This module aims to guide the management of these caseloads while maintaining a high standard of care. This module heavily focuses on the use of supervision to aid with this.

Knowledge will be learnt through a combination of lectures, seminars, reading and independent study. These skills will be put into practice almost immediately in service and therefore have a high focus on practical skills development.

This module will be assessed with a mixture of OSCEs, essays and recordings based on conducting a session with diverse patient groups. You will also be asked to continue to complete a portfolio demonstrating hours worked, and three written outcomes regarding your practice. This will be supervised by your service supervisor and marked by the university.

This part of the guide will focus on:
1. Cultural Competence
2. Biases and assumptions
3. The effective use of supervision
4. Treatment adaptations

Interview Tip: Most of the information from module three will not be needed for the interview.

Cultural Competence:

Interview Tip: This will not likely come up in an interview but it's good to be aware that one of the key aims of the NHS is to improve access to minority groups which are less likely to access NHS services.

Trainee Tips: This is a big part of the third module. Depending on where your service is based, you may have varying degrees of diversity. Regardless it is good to increase your knowledge of local cultures and improve your ability to engage any patients regardless of background.

What is Cultural Competence:
Cultural competence is the **awareness** of the socioeconomic and cultural factors involved in healthcare and the ability to work in a competence way with patients of various cultures.

Patient compliance and understanding of therapy is affected by socio-economic and social factors. Patients don't leave their beliefs at the door when they enter therapy, and neither does a therapist. Culture shapes our **behaviours and thoughts** and the way we **engage in healthcare**. This means that therapists need to be mindful of the social, cultural, and linguistic needs of each patient (and themselves) as these can influence the whole therapy process.

Why cultural competence is important:
Research has shown that cultural competence and cultural adaptations in healthcare is **essential to reduce ethnic disparities**, improve access and recovery. Ignoring cultural differences diminishes the ability to effectively communicate during sessions. This can reduce the therapeutic alliance and engagement in therapy. This is important as many studies have shown that ethnic minorities have poor health outcomes compared to white British populations, and are less likely to recover, receive or access support. This has been linked to many factors ranging from institutional racism, to social stigma.

Campinha-Bacote model of Cultural Competence:
One of the models used on the course is the Campinha-Bacote model. This is not the only way to view cultural competence and has its own set of drawbacks. There are various other models available.

Campinha-Bacote Model of Cultural Competence

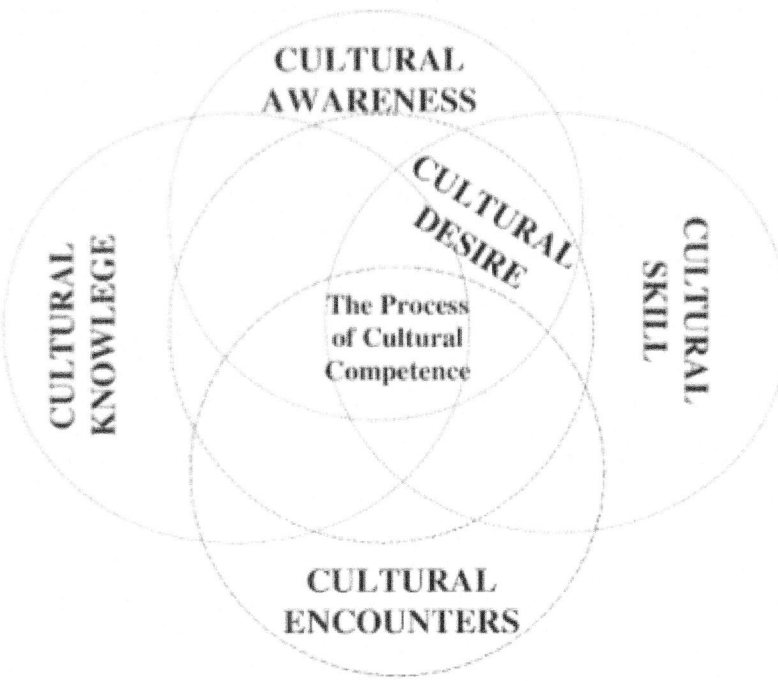

Figure 14: The Campinha-Bacote Model showing the overlapping 5 components of cultural competence.

The Campinha-Bacote model states that cultural competence is made up of five main constructs.

1. *Cultural Encounters:*
   Engaging in direct Cultural Encounters is the process that encourages engagement in patients from diverse backgrounds. This includes assessing and treating diverse populations. It can also include the use of interpreters to overcome any linguistic needs. The more cultural encounters that occur, the more opportunity you have to improve your competence.

2. *Cultural Skill:*
   Is the ability to collect relevant cultural data regarding the patients presenting problems as well as performing a culturally based assessment. This needs to examine the patient's individual, group and community beliefs, values and practices.

3. *Cultural Awareness:*
   Is the self-examination of one's own beliefs, culture, prejudices, assumptions and biases in regards to one's self and other cultures. If health care professionals are not aware of their own biases, they could impose their values onto their patients. It is best practice to make as few assumptions as possible. It is always best to ask the patient rather than assume something incorrectly.

4. *Cultural Desire:*
   Relates to your personal motivation to want to engage in other cultures, compared to just simply having too. Simply being aware and respecting a patient's values, beliefs and practises is not sufficient. You also need to show you genuinely care and show an interest in learning more.

5. *Cultural Knowledge*:

    Is the process of knowing about a culture, seeking additional information and education about various diverse cultural groups. It is okay to let a patient know that you don't know much or even anything about their culture. Explore that together with the patient to learn more. For health care providers, understanding the health related beliefs, values and the views of illness and treatment within a cultural group is important. Understanding the patient's view of mental health and treatment based on their culture is important: Find out what the patient feels their problem is. Some cultures don't even have words for some mental health disorders and view them differently. Consider if the patient's viewpoint clashes with CBT in any way?; What does their culture feel about reaching out for support?

Considerations for cultural competence:

- Therapists can work in a culturally sensitive way without a comprehensive training based on cultural competence guidance. This means you don't need to know all about a culture to work in a culturally competent way.
- Cultural-Competence is a continual, ongoing process and involves the interplay of cultural awareness, knowledge, skill, and desire. Cultural competence is a process, not an event; it lies on a spectrum and no one can fully say they are completely culturally competent.
- There is more variation within ethnic groups than across ethnic groups. So avoid assumptions based on your general knowledge of a group.
- There is a direct relationship between the level of competence of health care providers and their ability to provide culturally competent care.
- Cultural competence is an essential component in rendering effective and culturally responsive services to culturally and ethnically diverse clients.
- Cultural Competence is collaboration with the patient: Always consider treatment to be *"with the patient"*. Get their opinions and ideas rather than be prescriptive with treatment. This applies to all patients regardless of diversity.
- Cultural identification: Not all patients desire to connect or identify with their culture or heritage. This is important to consider to reduce the risk of making assumptions of the patient's culture. It can be useful to directly ask the patient what their culture is. This can also apply to subcultures.
- Also dont assume a diverse patient will need adaptations just because you perceive them to be from an enthic group.
- Dont assume a patient who struggles with English will want an interpreter. It can sometimes offend a patient as it shows you believe their ability to communicate is reduced. They might even be proud of their ability to speak english.

Unconscious Biases:

Everyone has biases. It is human nature to make assumptions and create mental heuristics to improve our cognitive speed (at a cost of accuracy). It is best to see biases as blindspots similar to those when driving. We don't see these blind spots clearly. But because we know they are there we can identify them and take intentional steps to mitigate their impact.

Often when people think of biases they may think of racism and hate. However, most biases are more subtle and can cause prejudices and impact for which we don't notice. Imagine having a belief that old people struggle with computers. This can often be correct, however, imagine if that stops you offering online or computerised CBT to that patient group. They will have less treatment options based on your assumption which may be incorrect for any particular individual. It could be the case that your particular elderly patient could have been a computer programmer and was one of the first users of the internet and have more experience than you. I have had many eldery patients prefer online therapy and young people who decline it.

The first step in this is identifying these biases. Often they can be hidden. Just asking yourself "what are my biases?", will often only identify surface level biases. But it is a good place to start.

It is also possible to complete online Implicit Association Tests (IAT) to help uncover any biases. These simple tests record your reaction time to answering questions. Biases work quicker than rational thought. So quicker answers can show areas in which you have a bias or stereotype.

Common Biases for Therapists:

Language:
- Do you have any biases about working with those who speak differently or struggle with the same language as you?
- Do you not like using interpreters in sessions?
- What about this makes you uncomfortable?

Age:
- Do you have any assumptions about age? Eg. Do you avoid offering computerised CBT to the elderly.
- Why?

Gender:
- Do you struggle to engage a certain gender?
- Do you know enough about gender related issues?
- Do you feel uncomfortable discussing gender with non gender binary patients?

Sexuality:
- Do you struggle or have any biases around a person's sexuality?

Race:
- Do you find it hard to work with or understand certain races?
- This isn't to say you are racist for struggling with other races different than yourself. But what is causing you to feel that way?

Stereotypes:
- Do you have any stereotypes about the patient?

Religion:
- If you are an atheist or working with a religion opposed to your own. How can you manage this? Imagine doing BA with that religion, focused on getting them to engage back with their religion.
- Would that cause you any moral dilemmas? Or would you judge a patient for losing their faith if it was the same as your own and feel it is your role to bring them back into the faith.

"Difficult Patients":
- Often it can be easy to put blame onto a patient for not being engaged or for causing a more difficult session. This is always worth exploring.
- It is your job to adapt to the patient, not for the patient to fit your view of an ideal patient.

"None Engaged Patients":
- Same as above. It can be easy to see the patient as simply non engaged "just because".
- Explore the barriers and find out what it is about treatment that is causing the non-engagement.

Your bias for a treatment plan:
- Do you believe one treatment is better than another?
- Do you struggle or dislike a treatment option?
- Do you try to only offer your preference to patients?
- Do you not offer face to face sessions as telephone is easier?

The list of biases can go on forever. Your biases can also change over time. Always try to be aware of your own biases. Attempt to seek out and attend workshops and seminars on unconscious bias. Engage in and consider initiating dialogue about implicit bias with your coworkers or other therapists. Clinical skills or case management supervision is a good place to discuss this

One of the best ways to identify biases is to focus on your emotional state prior, during or after working with a patient. Should you be feeling any negative emotions, that is a red flag to explore why you feel this way. What is it about the patient, the situation or yourself which is making you uncomfortable?

Treatment Adaptations:

Adapting treatment around a patient's cultural, health or other needs is important for effective therapy. There are too many treatment adaptations to detail all of them here. Adaptations should always be made on the patient's individual needs. Use supervision to discuss any changes made. As adaptations can sometimes bring the treatment away from its effective evidence base.

Interview: This is not needed for the interview.

Some typical adaptations include:

Language barriers:
- Use more simple terminology to aid with understanding.
- Avoid metaphors and idioms which are only understood by native english speakers.
- Use translated materials.
- Use an interpreter if needed.

Material Selection:
- The use of materials is paramount for guided self help. Deciding what guide to use is very important.
- If you had a patient who struggles to read, then sending them a larger 40 page guide might be a barrier. Consider the length of the guide used.
- More motivated patients may prefer the larger guide.

Speed:
- The speed of the session needs to vary based on the patient's understanding.
- Go at the pace of the patient.
- Some patients will have the capacity to learn the whole intervention in one session, while others will need to spaced out over multiple sessions.

Time:
- Some patients may need more time in sessions to comprehend the materials.
- You can either offer more sessions or change the length.

Metaphors:
- Metaphors can be a good way to engage patients.
- Consider their use when patients are struggling to understand the treatment.

Long Term Health Conditions:
- Adaptations need to be made for patients with long term health conditions.
- The adaptation will depend on the condition. However, two commonly used techniques are pacing and the SOC model. Both of these are described below.

Pacing:

Pacing is a technique used (often alongside BA) for when a patient is experiencing pain or fatigue. Typically they can be trapped in what is called a **"boom and bust"** cycle where they overdo their activities then have negative physical consequences which reduce their activity level while recovering. This is usually for chronic fatigue and fibromyalgia. More recently this has become ever more relevant due to the new condition of long covid.

Below are the two cycles which show how this occurs for pain and fatigue. The cycle is basically identical for both.

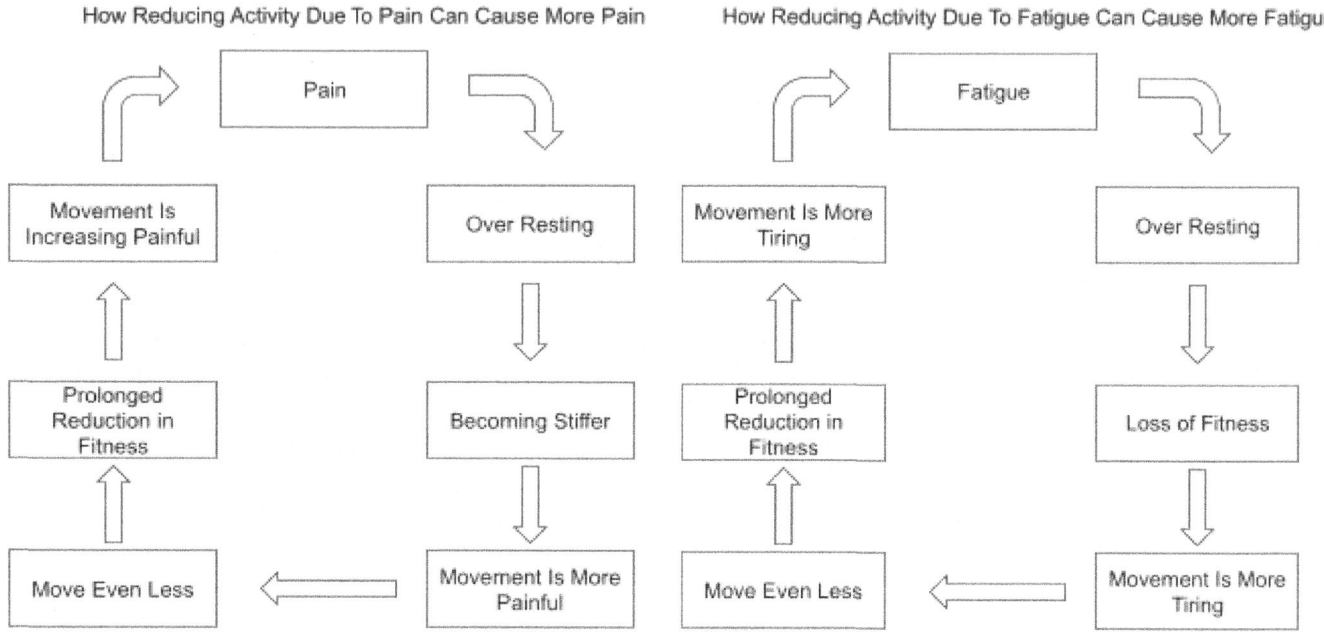

Figure 15 : Pain Vicious Cycle   **Figure 16 : Fatigue Vicious Cycle**

As you can see, both pain and fatigue cause a reduction in physical activity. Over a prolonged time this can reduce muscle strength and lead to a loss of fitness. Which reduces activity levels. And based on the depression formulation, can lead to depression. This naturally makes activity harder which compounds this effect as it causes more pain and fatigue which starts the cycle again.

When an individual is in this cycle they can attempt to capitalise on "good days" where they have less pain and fatigue. This causes a "Boom and Bust Cycle". Below is a typical boom and bust situation.

Boom and Bust Cycle

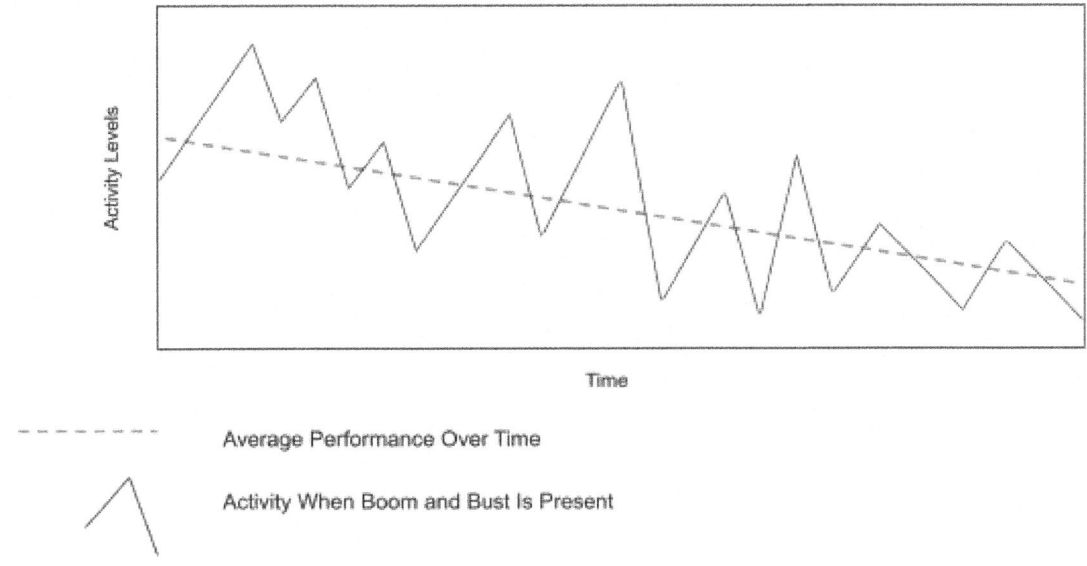

– – – – – – – –   Average Performance Over Time

Activity When Boom and Bust Is Present

Figure 17 : Boom and Bust Vicious Cycle; Which Shows That Baseline Performance Reduces Overtime.

This "Boom and Bust" diagram shows the typical performance of someone who has chronic pain or fatigue. When they experience **pain or fatigue** they naturally **do less** as activity is **more difficult**. This can often cause a **backlog of tasks** and they can become **guilty** or feel "lazy". When a day occurs when they feel better, they attempt to **"make up for lost time"** and try to do much more activity. This causes their **performance to spike**. However, this causes their condition to **flare up**. Then their performance for the next few days **decreases as they need to rest and recover**. This can lead further into the symptoms of feeling guilty and low. So the cycle continues, each time getting worse. Over time **performance can dip lower than when they started**, even on "good days".

The treatment to this is to introduce **pacing**. The next diagram shows that performance when pacing is introduced may be lower than the patients typical activity level. However, it **increases over time** rather than reduces as seen with boom and bust.

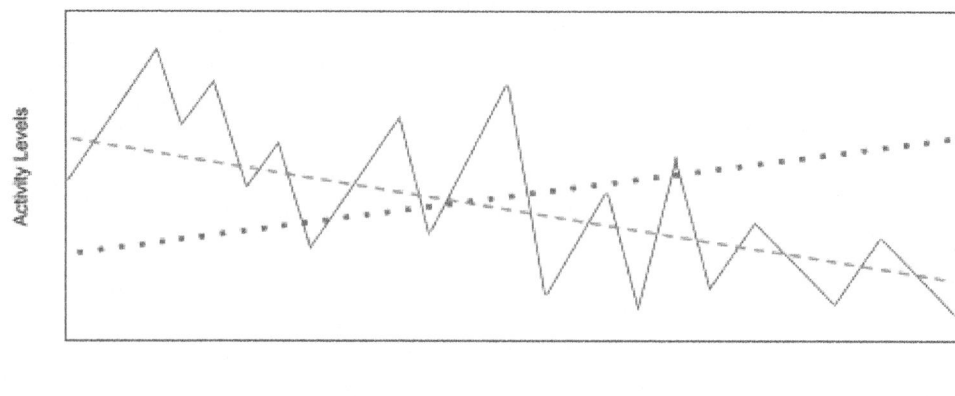

Boom and Bust
Vs Pacing

- - - - - - - Average Performance Over Time During
            Boom and Bust.

            Activity When Boom and Bust Is Present.

· · · · · Average Activity When Pacing

Figure 18 : Pacing Performance; Which Shows That Baseline Performance Can Increase Overtime compared to Boom and Busting.

What is Pacing?

Pacing is a skill that aims to allow a person to **consistently carry out their activities** without causing pain or fatigue. It aims to **neither over exert** or **over rest**. Therefore, a patient needs to figure out how long to spend on an activity to get the most out of it, without overdoing it. Over time this amount of time during an activity can increase as the patient becomes more physically able.

How to work out the correct time?

1) Choose an activity.
2) The patient then needs to do the activity and **stop when any pain or fatigue occurs**. This should be done at least three times on both good and bad days.
3) Record the length of time for **each attempt**.
4) Take the **average** of all of these times. Then **subtract a fifth.**

This gives the patient an accurate time in which the patient should be able to do their activity free of pain and fatigue. The patient needs to stick to this time and try not to overexert themselves. This can involve stopping a task before finishing. That is okay and advised.
If it is an activity that needs completing and stopping would be difficult (such as cooking), then it is advised to discuss how to break down the task into sections so that it can still be completed without going over time.

Example:

Time 1	Time 2	Time 3	Time 4	Average	Average Minus 1/5th
10m	15m	11m	9m	11.25m	9m

SOC (Selection, Optimization, and Compensation) Model:

One of the adaptations taught on the course is the SOC model. This strategy is often aimed towards eldery patients who are struggling with age related functional decline. But it also applies to anyone who has suffered a loss of ability in life. SOC stands for "Selection, Optimization, and Compensation. When faced with a **loss of ability**, a person's goals in life can **exceed their new ability**. Therefore it is important to **reduce the demands** or **improve coping**. This can occur in three main ways (Selection, Optimization, and Compensation).

Selection:
Selection refers to developing and committing to personal goals and values. Achieving goals contributes to feeling that one's life has a purpose. In life there are endless goals to pursue. This number of goals far exceeds our abilities in terms of internal (motivation, capability etc.) and external (opportunity; time; money etc.) resources. Therefore, we need to **select** and **focus** on the goals which are **important for us** to achieve.

There are two types of selection:

Elective Selection: Aiming to **voluntarily** reduce the amount of expectations in certain areas to improve and focus on achievement in a particular few.

Loss-based Selection: Reducing expectations in areas we are eve **due to loss of ability** to achieve (e.g. Due to illness, injury or age).no longer able to achi

Here are some example goals and values patients often focus on and some questions to help patients identify how they fit within each category.
1. Family:
   - What type of relationships do you want to have?
   - What sort of brother/sister, mother/father, uncle/aunt etc do I want to be?
   - What kind of partner do I want to be?
2. Social:
   - What type of friend do you want to be?
   - How often do I want to see my friends?
   - What type of friendships are important for me?
   - What could I do to improve my friendships?
3. Career:
   - What type of work is important to me?
   - What qualities do I want to bring into work?
   - What time of relationships do I want at work?
   - What can I bring/improve in my workplace?
4. Fun:
   - How would you like to enjoy yourself?
   - What hobbies do I enjoy?
   - What have I always wanted to try?
   - What relaxes me?
   - What do I find fun?
   - What do I enjoy doing with others?
5. Spirituality:
   - What relationship do you want with your faith?

- What can I do to enhance myself spiritually?
- What kind of relationship do I want with my god/s.
6. Health:
- What can I do to improve my physical or mental health?
- How can I care for myself better?
- Should I stop smoking, drinking or taking drugs?

The aim of this is to get the patient to consider what activity/role/hobby they want to focus on. Consider SMART goals to aid with this.

Optimisation:
Optimisation refers to **improving our abilities** to achieve our desired goal. This often is in the form of time and effort. The aim is to refine our ability to achieve a goal.

Get the patient to think about what they can do to improve their selected Goal/Value. What do they need to practice or do differently?. This pairs up nicely with a BA diary to start scheduling in practice.

Compensation:
Compensation is the giving up of **unattainable goals** and **replacing them** for **attainable goals**, or by investing in the optimisation of already existing goals.
The **maintenance of functioning** in the face of losses is important for growth and mental well being.
Accepting the reality of a loss does not mean a person has to put up with losing something they value. It can also mean you can instead work on **finding a new way to keep these values/goals in their life.**

Some helpful questions to get the patient to reflect on:
- What am I currently unable to do? and what could I be doing differently with my time?
- What aspects of my goals can I achieve?
- What aspects am I currently unable to achieve?
- How else could I be spending my time and effort?
- Are there any approaches, tools or technologies that can help me achieve my goal?

Barriers and COM-B:

Interview Tip:

- *COM-B is not required for the interview. This is a recent addition to the PWP course so if the interviewer qualified years ago then they may not know much about this themselves.*

There are many barriers to effective treatment sessions. We have covered many of these during each individual treatment section. This section will go over some of the most common ones that can occur and provide some advice on how to overcome them. There are many more barriers than these. Therefore, we will focus on the ability to solve them which can be applied to any barriers not covered here.

The model used within IAPT to overcome most barriers is called the COM-B Model. The model is more advanced than this guide will go into. Therefore, some external reading on the topic is advised. COM-B is an acronym for "capability", "opportunity", "motivation" and "behaviour". It states that for any effective behaviour change there are three components (capability, opportunity, and motivation').

COM-B

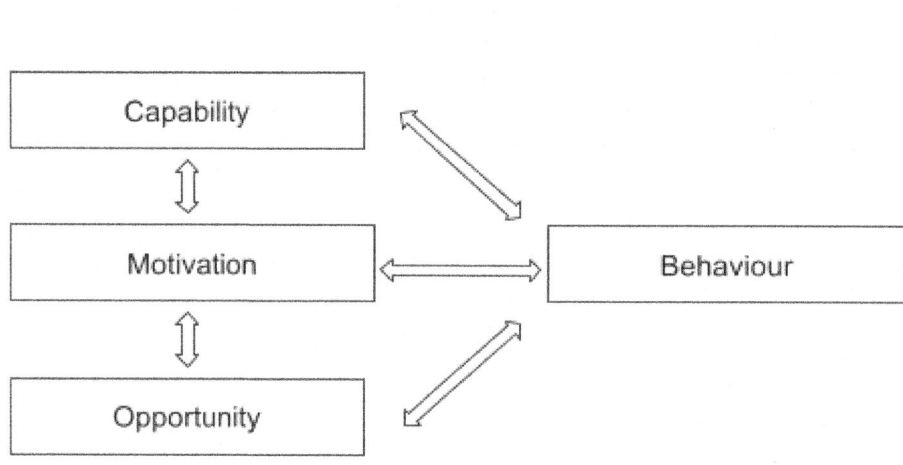

Figure 19: COM-B Model Which Shows The Three Main Components For Behavioural Change.

As you can see from the multi-directional arrows on the diagram. These factors all influence each other. So positive change in just one area can lead to changes elsewhere.

Capability refers to an individual's psychological and physical capacity to engage in change. This can involve:
- Knowledge
- Skills
- Mental capacity (eg. struggling after a stroke)
- Physical capacity (eg. injury)

Motivation refers to an individual having all the brain processes that energise and direct behaviour. This is not just a person's goals and conscious decision making but accounts for their ability to regulate their physical energy (eg. imagine a depressed patient who knows what they need to do; but it doesn't mean they have the energy or act on it) .

- Does the patient want to change?
- Is the patient willing to try (eg. exposure is scary and requires a patient to engage in their feared situation)?
- Does the patient have the reflective processes for change (plans and evaluations)?
- Does the patient have the automatic processes needed (emotions, impulses and patterns learnt)?
- Does the patient have "learned helplessness"?

Opportunity refers to all the factors outside of an individual's control which makes behaviour change possible or impossible.

- Social Opportunities (eg. A patient may want to spend time with friends; Do they have any social opportunities for this or not)
- Environmental Opportunities (eg. If a patient's goal is to swim more; do they have access to a pool or not)
- Financial (eg. Can the patient afford the change?)

Behaviour in the model refers to any behaviour change both in or outside of the session. This can also relate to any other behaviour too:

- Engagement in Homework.
- Turning up to sessions.
- Reading the materials.

This model can be very useful to consider both at the IA stage and the treatment stage. One of the sections of the IA is looking at barriers to treatment. Consider briefly exploring COM-B with the patient. This can be useful in the shared decision making process.

For example; if a patient likes the idea of doing cognitive restructuring but after exploring barriers they state they are not able to write well, or that they have constant mental fog. Then a conversation about how to overcome these prior to starting CR, or maybe discussing why CR might be less effective than BA in this case can be had with the patient.

This model also is important during treatments. For all the barriers below, consider how and if COM-B can be used. There is no right answer and every patient/situation can be different. So these are just examples. Use your own judgement. Learning to explore barriers collaboratively is key.

Non-engagement: Some patients will not be engaged in the treatment. They may appear not interactive, or you may just get a sense that they are not engaged. This is a good opportunity to explore this with the patient.

- Ask them how they are finding the sessions?
- Is there anything they are struggling with?
- Is there anything we can change about the sessions to help?
- Explore the capability', 'opportunity', and 'motivation' of the patient.

Over talkative patients: Some patients will come into CBT with the expectation that it is like counselling. They may want to talk about their problems rather than learn strategies. This can lead to some patients who go on long tangents or tell their life stories.

- This relates to the capability section. Dont assume the patient has the knowledge to be aware that this is not how guided self help works. Discuss with the patient the advantages of telling the life stories (often short term reassurance) compared to spending the sessions as they were intended to get a longer term benefit.
- Should a patient want to spend the sessions talking then refer or signpost to counselling.
- Always link the patient's experience back to the material (if appropriate). The ABC cycle is great for this: Eg. "I hear what you are saying, it sounds like that was a tough situation for you [Or any other empathy statement]. It might be a good idea if we try to apply that situation to the ABC cycle".
- Often PWP's can feel uncomfortable or even rude interrupting patients. Reflect on this and if you have any biases to overcome. Often being structured is actually in the best interest of the patient to reach recovery. It may not feel nice, but by allowing the patient too much time to talk, you may be reducing the effectiveness of the therapy for the patient.
- Get comfortable "containing" patients using statements such as "I am just aware of time". Make sure this is appropriate as if used incorrectly this can still be rude or inconsiderate.
- The exception to containing the patient is for patients who have long term health conditions or chronic pain. Often these patients have been passed around the healthcare system multiple times and may have felt unheard. It can be useful to book a longer appointment and allow them some time to talk. But do remain structured and to the materials as much as possible. Balance is key.

Non talkers: Some patients will be very quiet. This often occurs with depressed patients. This can feel a bit awkward for PWP's (reflect on why).
- Explore how the patient is finding the sessions.
- This could relate to the patient's motivation. They may want to engage but not have the brain processing abilities.
- Discuss this openly with patients. They could be struggling with something. They could be struggling to open up. They might be shy. It is worth exploring and can actually lead to a more collaborative treatment.
- Double check their understanding. Often patients with low self esteem or anxieties may sit in silence when they can't follow a conversation as they feel they can't ask questions.
- Ask open questions to get them to talk.
- Sometimes saying nothing and just waiting for a response can prompt them to answer or expand.

Not doing homework. Often patients will not do their homework outside of sessions. This can greatly reduce recovery rates.
- Explore using COM-B if there was a cause. Get the patient to overcome those barriers.
- Reinforce why doing the work is needed for change.
- Explore if it is the right time for therapy. Sometimes patients are not ready to engage.

Patient states they have no time for homework: This relates to all three areas of COM-B.
- Get the patient to realise how prioritising their homework is key.
- Explore how to make the time.
- Often the patient actually have the time. But not the motivation or skills to use it effectively.
- Explore if it is the right time for therapy. Sometimes patients are not ready to engage.

Patient not understanding the treatment: Some patients may be confused about how to do the treatment, any of the psychoeducation points or about the rationale.
- Slow down.
- Get the patient to tell you their understanding from the beginning. Correct any mistakes

- Consider their capacity.
- Consider changing how you deliver the content for this patient. One style will not work with everyone.
- Use metaphors as this can help aid understanding.
- Switch treatments if needed. I have had patients who just couldn't get their head around CR but found BA really easy.

Not willing to try: Some patients may perceive the strategy silly, basic or not what they were expecting, or for some reason be unwilling to try it.
- Explore if it is the right time for therapy. Sometimes patients are not ready to engage.
- Explore what about the strategy they do not like? Have they misunderstood something?
- Patients can sometimes see problem solving as obvious, BA as too basic, worrytime as strange, cognitive restructuring as confusing and exposure as scary. Overcome these barriers.
- They might have wanted counselling rather than CBT.
- Look at the patient's motivation for change.
- Get them to see the benefits of trying the strategy; it working vs the small loss of some time for giving it a go.

"Complex" Patients: At times you will be assigned a patient who is too complex for step 2. This can be due to many factors from it being missed at the IA, or step 3 waiting lists becoming too long and the service starting patients on step 2.
- Focus on what you can help the patient with. You don't have to completely cure a patient. Set a SMART goal. Remember a key part is "achievable". Focus on what you can achieve at step 2.
- Avoid drifting away from the evidence base. Do not attempt step 3 work.
- Do not face complexity with complexity. Stick to one intervention. Go simple.
- Take to supervision.

Cancelling sessions with excuses: (This will depend on your individual service policies) During treatment some patients will cancel regularly with what sound like good excuses.
- Explore if it is the right time for therapy. Sometimes patients are not ready to engage.
- Inform the patient of the service policy about missing appointments. Attendance requires commitment.
- Explore if there are any barriers to the sessions. Motivation for depression or is there any anxiety stopping the patient.
- Reinforce that CBT is only effective if the patient does it.

Barriers don't just occur on the side of the patient. Therapists also have barriers to providing quality care. In the third module of the course you will explore these barriers and uncover any bias you may have. You can also apply COM-B to yourself.

Trainee Tip: My best advice for this is that if you ever look at your calendar for the day and have a certain patient that you dread seeing or have any sort of negative response too. Then that is a red flag to reflect on what is causing you to have that response. You are not a bad therapist or person. Everyone has had that response at some point. But it is important to know why. What is it about that patient's case that is causing your discomfort?
1. Is it the patient?
    - Do you consider them rude, non engaged, "difficult" in some way, challenging?

- Is there a bias you have (eg. they are an eldery patient and you consider those cases harder)?
- Is it a complex case?

2. Is it the treatment?
    - Is it not working?
    - Do you not like a particular intervention?
    - Are you struggling to apply it to the patient?
    - Are you drifting from the evidence base and feel out of your depth or stuck?

3. Is it something about yourself?
    - Do you feel you are failing with this patient?
    - Do you think it's going to be a hard session?
    - Are you ill? Burnt-out?
    - Do you feel out of your depth or not confident in something?
    - Is your motivation or capacity reduced for whatever reason?

This is important in becoming a reflective practitioner. There is a reason the university course spends so much time getting you to reflect on yourself. Biases are natural. But you need to be aware of them and overcome them to be the best therapist you can be. This is a continual process. If you notice any of these issues, you can always bring it to clinical skills or case management supervision. You will probably not be alone in feeling this way.

Trainee Tip:
- *Never get into the habit of overcoming the patient's barriers for them. This robs them of the chance for self discovery and to overcome their own barriers.*
- *It is always best to ask the patient if they can think of any ways to overcome their issue first.*
- *Even if they are struggling, guide them towards answers rather than telling them directly.*
- *Always! always! always! always! reflect on yourself. __Don't let this stop after the university course ends.__ Review what you are doing well, what you are not. Have you drifted from best practice? If you have stopped doing something (eg. the problem statement) why?*
- *As time goes on, PWP's tend to become less collaborative in sessions. This naturally occurs as the job is so repetitive. They can start "teaching" the material rather than using the collaborative style the university teaches. Be aware of this drift and make aims to continually improve your collaboration.*
- *Be aware of any drift. Imagine your sessions are being recorded and marked by your lecturer. Would you still pass your OSCE? If not, why not try to return to best practice.*

Supervision:

Supervision is the process of reflection and review which enables PWPs to increase individual self-awareness, develop their competences and improve quality of care for patients.
There are two types:
- **Case Management** supervision where you discuss your cases with your supervisor on a weekly basis.
- **Clinical Skills** which occur for at least once a month for up to 2 hours. This is usually a group supervision with other PWPs.

Supervision has three major functions. Often called the "Normative", "Restorative" and "Formative" functions:

Normative:
- The normative function focuses on quality assurance, ethical practice and patient protection. This involves reviewing cases and ensuring risk is being managed effectively.

Restorative:
- The restorative function is aimed to reduce staff burn out. It gives the space for the supervisee to discuss any concerns they are having.

Formative:
- The formative function is about the improvement of knowledge, skills and abilities.

Case Management Supervision:

Case Management Supervision will be provided **weekly** and consist of a minimum of one hour a week of individual supervision.

During this time you will go through certain aspects of your **caseload and discuss patients** with your supervisor. The aim is to review all clinical cases routinely.

The purpose of supervision:
- For the supervisor to have **insight into your clinical practice** being conducted to ensure safe practice for patients.
- **Improve** and **develop** therapeutic skills
- **Fidelity to the evidence base**: All PWPs need to be able to carry out the same intervention and to the same level of competence.
- Effective Case management and collaborative care: **Cases need to be reviewed** at least every 4 weeks and **step ups need to be discussed**. This process ensures **no patients get overlooked**.
- Dealing with individual cases and ensuring **safe practice**: All patients should be discussed to ensure that you have not missed anything and that the patient is receiving the correct psychological therapy.
- Difficult cases should be discussed for advice.
- Reviewing Risk: Cases need to be **reviewed for risk** to ensure all necessary steps are being taken to **manage any active risk**.
- Staff support: Supervision is designed to help **stop therapist burn out**. The PWP job can be intense and any concerns need to be raised and addressed. Therapists are not immune to personal issues or negative past events. Sometimes these personal issues can be echoed by

patients and can cause psychological distress to the therapist. Supervision can also ensure you are currently fit to practice or help you overcome any barriers you are currently facing.

Clinical Skills Supervision:

Clinical Skills Supervision is less frequent than case management. It usually occurs at least once a month for up to 2 hours. This supervision is focused on the **development and maintenance** of your **competence** and occurs in a group setting. It gives you a chance to discuss cases. Occasionally they can act as teaching opportunities on various CBT techniques.

The purpose of Clinical Skills Supervision:
- Maintenance of competence.
- Improve and develop therapeutic skills
- Reduce drift from the evidence base
- Get advice on cases

 *Interview Tips:*
- *You may get a question about what you know about IAPT or being a PWP. This is a great place to discuss your knowledge of supervision.*

The Basics:
- *Case management supervision is to manage caseload and discuss patients*
- *Clinical Skills is about maintaining and developing your clinical skills.*

Should be easy to remember; It's in the name.

 *Trainee Tips:*
- *Have cases prepared for supervision. Both the supervisor and yourself have a responsibility to prepare prior to supervision.*
- *At a full caseload you will have a lot of cases to discuss in every supervision. Practice various methods and speak to other PWP's in your service on how they manage this time pressure. Find what works for you.*
- *Don't be afraid to let your supervisor know if you are struggling with something. The point of supervision is to help overcome any issues.*
- *Think of Cases to bring to Clinical Skills. It's a great place to get and give advice.*
- *Be aware of abusive supervision. Hopefully this should never occur. But if you are having any issues. Do raise them with your supervisor, manager, or with your course lecturers.*

University Portfolio:

Interview Tip:
You do not need to know about this for the interview at all. But it can show you have looked into the job in detail. Knowing what will be required after you get the job is useful for your own knowledge.

Portfolio: Throughout each module you will be expected to keep a portfolio to record your clinical work in service. This includes reflective outcomes on your performance. This will be marked by the university who will also liaise with your service to ensure you are working competently with patients.

Each university has differences in the portfolio so this may vary.

The portfolio is comprised of [subject to change by the university]:
- A supervision contract.
- A brief training contract that details your learning objectives.
- A log of all case management supervisions with dates, hours logged and signed by your supervisor.
- A log of all clinical skills supervisions with dates, hours logged and signed by your supervisor.
- A log of all clinical contacts with patients including the type of contact (assessment or treatment), contact time, and supervisor signatures for each.
- A record of all study days taken.
- A log of roleplays observed by the university.
- A reflective log of each case management supervision. Including the date, what was discussed, learnt and any actions for future learning and how past actions were completed.
- A reflective log of each clinical skills management supervision. Including the date, what was discussed, learnt and any actions for future learning and how past actions were completed.

Module 1:
- 1-3 Anonymised Clinical Notes. Signed and approved by supervisor
- Multiple assessments observed, signed and approved by supervisor
- Outcome essays on your practice. Signed and approved by supervisor

Module 2:
- Outcome essays on your practice of treatment. Signed and approved by supervisor

Module 3:
- Outcome essays on your practice on diversity and the use of supervision. Signed and approved by supervisor

Trainee Tip:
- *Do not let the portfolio pile up. Complete it weekly. Nothing is worse than trying to remember and document what you discussed and learnt 7 supervisons ago.*
- *Also collect your supervisor's signatures as you go along. No supervisor wants to sign 100 things the week before a deadline.*
- *The outcome essays are about your performance in practice. This requires writing in a reflective way. This is very different from essay writing you may have done at university. Most students try*

to write these descriptively about how an assessment or treatment is done. This is incorrect. It's about how **you** do your assessments and treatments.

Module Three Summary:

This concludes the information for chapter three.
By this point you should have as good idea regarding:

- Why it is important to be inclusive of diversity
- What cultural Competence is
- A brief understanding of what biases are
- Treatment adaptations including pacing and the SOC model
- How to use the COM-B model to assess and overcome barriers
- What supervision is
- A bit about the portfolio for university

Interview Stage: As mentioned before you are not expected to know much about this module. If you get any questions about the trust or NHS values in your interview it might be good to mention cultural competence and being inclusive of diversity.

Trainee Before Module Three: Module three tends to be seen as the easiest as you will not be learning as much as the last two modules. It is a good time to consolidate all the knowledge you have acquired. It is good to think on your biases a bit before the lectures begin. Be prepared for the increase in your caseload which will be coming soon.

Trainee After Module Three: Hopefully you found the university lecture very informative and interesting. Always continue to reflect on your biases and competence. Good luck with the last stage of your training and becoming qualified.

The End:

I hope you have found this guide helpful.

Should this guide help you get your job or survive the course please consider leaving a review

Printed in Great Britain
by Amazon

41665946R00084